MW01482325

Roll of the Dice

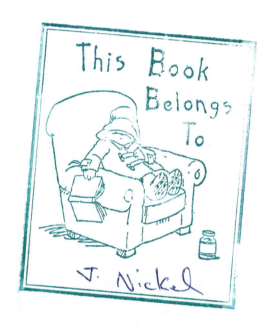

Roll of the Dice

Working with Clyde Wells
during the Meech Lake Negotiations

Deborah Coyne

James Lorimer & Company, Publishers
Toronto 1992

Copyright ©1992 James Lorimer & Company, Publishers

All rights reserved. No part of this book may be reproduced or transmitted in any form or by any means, electronic or mechanical, including photocopying, or by any information storage and retrieval system, without permission in writing from the publisher.

Canadian Cataloguing in Publication Data
Coyne, Deborah M.R. (Deborah Margaret Ryland),
1955-
   Roll of the Dice

Includes index.
ISBN 1-55028-371-5 (bound) ISBN 1-55028-369-3 (pbk.)

1. Meech Lake Constitutional Accord (1987).
2. Wells, Clyde K., 1937-   . 3. Canada - Constitutional law - Amendments. 4. Canada - Constitutional history. 5. Federal-provincial relations - Canada.*   6. Canada - Politics and government - 1984-   . I. Title.

JL65 1992 C68 1992   342.71'03   C92-093754-3

Cover photograph of dice: Julian Beveridge
Author photograph: Michael Bedord

James Lorimer & Company, Publishers
Egerton Ryerson Memorial Building
35 Britain Street
Toronto, Ontario
M5A 1R7

Printed and bound in Canada

CONTENTS

INTRODUCTION

ON THE AFTERNOON of Friday, June 22, 1990, I was almost certain that the Meech Lake constitutional accord was dead when the premier of Newfoundland and Labrador stood in the House of Assembly to adjourn the debate. But I was not convinced until I heard the federal minister of state for federal-provincial relations, Senator Lowell Murray, pronounce its death later that evening. And even then I did not start to unwind until after the prime minister addressed the nation the next day. This event marked the end of an exhausting and often painful process that had begun in May 1987.

This book is about my involvement in the Meech Lake constitutional debate as the constitutional advisor to Premier Clyde Wells of Newfoundland. It covers the critical period from October 1989 to June 1990. I have written it for a number of reasons. First, I hope that my perspective as an outsider and then an insider in the constitutional reform process will contribute some valuable insights both in assessing what happened and in identifying lessons for the future. More specifically, I hope it will show the fundamental flaws in the closed-door intergovernmental approach to constitutional reform and emphasize the urgent need to open up the process through meaningful public hearings combined with a referendum.

Second, I want to reveal the depth of constructive public concern with the Accord from the earliest days. I want to demonstrate how, despite the cynical manipulation by certain key politicians and others, despite the failure of the nation's parliamentary opposition, and despite the absence of any national leadership, the voice of the people was heard and

ultimately prevailed. This means that we have reason to be optimistic for Canada's future. If the *people* of Canada want the
country to hold together, if the *people* of Canada believe in a coherent national government and national leadership that will
inspire us to pursue our ideal of a bilingual, multicultural nation and a fairer, more compassionate society, then we must let
the *people* into the process and allow them to influence constitutional reforms in a meaningful way.

Premier Wells's greatest contributions to the debate were
his principles and his commitment to open up the process to
the widest possible public involvement. What he recognized
was that the vast majority of Canadians believe that constitutional reform should reflect an underlying set of principles on
which there is consensus. Reform should not be treated as a
partisan political game of manipulation and trade-offs, carried
out behind closed doors. In standing up to Brian Mulroney
and his "roll of the dice" approach, Wells inspired millions of
Canadians and restored people's faith in politicians. For a period of time, he provided the national leadership so
desperately lacking in our era of cynical politics.

As we now engage in another intense round of constitutional discussions, it does not appear that the lessons of the
Meech experience have been learned. Of course, there have
been endless commissions, committees, and conferences. But
the federal government has now entered a phase of behind-
the-scenes deal making with provincial premiers and refuses
to submit the new reforms to the ultimate test of public opinion — a national referendum (although not foreclosing it as a
desperate measure in the event of a deadlock with the provinces). More important, we have been put back in the grip of
another manufactured constitutional crisis. For some time
now, the prime minister and his lieutenants have been cranking
up their brinkmanship strategy and repeating the now-familiar
apocalyptic refrain that the moment of constitutional truth has
arrived and that we will have to accept the constitutional deal
or lose everything — our international reputation, our heritage, Canada itself. This is the ultimate "roll of the dice"
strategy, and it remains to be seen if Canadians will this time
succumb to it — if only out of fatigue. I hope not.

The current proposals have essentially all the same elements of the Meech Lake Accord, with Senate reform, a tooth-
less social covenant, and aboriginal self-government added to

buy off the opposition. Like Meech, they will never satisfy Quebec nationalists, who are the driving force behind Quebec's demands. All they will do is grant the Quebec government a significant chunk of the powers of a nation-state and whet its appetite for complete independence. It is difficult to believe that the vast numbers of Canadians who opposed Meech will now accept these proposals.

The Meech Lake Accord would have reversed our constitutional evolution of the last twenty years and taken the country in an entirely different direction. It would have granted Quebec special status by giving its government the power to preserve and promote its "distinct identity," a concept that could be interpreted to include a vast range of policy areas. This power would also have permitted the Quebec government to, in effect, override the Charter and justify infringements of individual and minority rights in order to promote the French-speaking majority. In a modern liberal democracy based on the inviolability of individual rights, this is unacceptable. And while it was granting these additional powers to the Quebec government, the Accord would have provided merely for the "preservation" of the English minority in Quebec and French minorities outside Quebec. At the very least, the prevailing vision of a bilingual nation required the *promotion* of such minorities across Canada by all governments, federal *and* provincial.

The other elements of the Accord would have resulted in a significant devolution of powers to the provinces and, in the view of many Canadians, an unacceptable weakening of the federal government. The federal government would no longer have been a truly national government directly representing the interests of all Canadians; it would have become merely an agent of the provincial governments. This is because the Accord provided for provincial control of appointments to the Supreme Court of Canada and the Senate, two *national* institutions which must be able to rise above narrow provincial interests and enunciate the broader national interest. The Accord also made the constitutional amending formula even more inflexible by extending the list of subjects requiring unanimous provincial consent and, at the same time, made it easier for provinces to opt out of all constitutional amendments that might give more legislative power to Parliament. The combined effect of these provisions would have been to give all provinces, notably Quebec, what amounted to a veto over all constitutional change. (Although a single province could not have stopped or vetoed changes to the division of powers, it would have had the right to declare that an amendment just didn't apply to it, and would not have suffered any adverse impact, since it would have received financial compensation.)

The federal government's power to spend in areas of exclusive provincial jurisdiction would have been severely limited. Any province would have had the right to opt out of any new shared-cost program with financial compensation; in return, it need only have complied with "the national objective." This would have made it almost impossible to launch major new national social programs to address the needs of the most vulnerable and disadvantaged and would have crippled any coherent effort to maintain minimum national standards.

The Accord would have allowed for bilateral agreements concerning immigration, the result being eleven different immigration policies and the virtual abandonment of the federal role. Finally, the Accord would have entrenched annual First Ministers' Conferences on the Constitution or any other matter, effectively creating a third, unaccountable level of government that was essentially controlled by the provinces.

The substance of the Accord did clearly respond to the Quebec government's five "demands." In effect, what Prime Minister Mulroney did was agree to all those demands and then, where appropriate, extend any concession to all the provinces in order to persuade them to agree. As so many critics were to ask: Who spoke for Canada in the negotiations?

The absence of a strong federal negotiator was only one of many fundamental problems. Equally serious was that the federal government propagated the myth that Quebec was somehow excluded from the Constitution in 1982 and that this exclusion justified significant concessions to "make the country whole again." Not only was this untrue, but it also bolstered the Quebec nationalist forces so that, as the Accord came under fire, they were able to play effectively to Quebeckers' emotions and argue that they were being rejected yet again.

Quebec has always been part of the Constitution of Canada. In 1982, the Supreme Court held, in a case instigated by the Parti Québécois government, that Quebec was still bound by the Constitution, as it had been since 1867, despite the refusal of the Quebec government to consent willingly to the constitutional reforms of 1982. Among many other things, this meant that all federal laws continued to apply in Quebec. In 1982 the separatist government of René Lévesque would not have agreed to anything that promoted the federation. At the same time, all but two of the federal MPs from Quebec voted in favour of the amendments.

Since then, pollster Angus Reid has convincingly demonstrated that the constitutional situation in Quebec was not of particular concern after 1982. For example, as of June 1986, almost 75 percent of Canadians supported official bilingualism and a number of Quebec polling firms had stopped asking questions on independence or separatism altogether.

Since there was no real urgency to resolve Quebec's position on the Constitution, the Meech Lake Accord took most observers by surprise when it was negotiated in 1987. The media, in their scramble to react, were so surprised that the first ministers had achieved unanimity that little or no criticism was made of the Accord's substance. The almost universal complacency with which the Accord was accepted was surprising. It was only questioned seriously in the lead editorials in the *Toronto Star* and *Saturday Night*.

A fundamental reason for this media collapse was the total failure of the national parliamentary opposition to criticize the Accord's substance in any serious way. Had there been any such debate, the media would have covered it, which would have given a crucial voice to the millions of Canadians who were genuinely concerned about the direction in which the Accord would take the nation.

In the end, the widespread opposition to the Accord was articulated through a variety of outlets and forums, and through a succession of new provincial premiers, Clyde Wells being the most prominent. For those who still say that the Meech Lake Accord was a good one and who argue that the opposition amounted to a mere 7 percent of the Canadian population in three small provinces, I challenge them, as Richard Gwyn also did in the *Toronto Star* on August 13, 1990, to read the over 30,000 letters that Premier Wells received between November 1989 and June 1990. As Gwyn notes perceptively, "They will find there the exposed nerve-ends of a nation." They will also find themselves asking why the Canadian body politic was put through such unnecessary pain. In the long term, the consequences of the Meech debate itself will be far more damaging than the fact that the Accord was rejected.

ONE

On the Inside

ON A SUNNY FRIDAY AFTERNOON in June 1989, I found myself standing in a dimly lit corridor of the Sheraton Centre in downtown Toronto, knocking on the door of a suite. Just the day before, I had received a telephone call from the office of Premier Clyde Wells in St. John's, Newfoundland, asking me if I was available for a meeting with the premier. I wasn't sure what to expect, but I had immediately said yes.

At the time, I was working as program director at the Walter Gordon Charitable Foundation, an organization that supported non-profit initiatives in the areas of peace and security and education and development in Canada's north. Before this, I had taught law and public policy at the University of Toronto. When the Meech Lake Accord was announced in 1987, I felt as if I had been hit by an acute allergy. In my view, the Accord amounted to a complete reversal of our constitutional evolution and, despite the apparent unanimous support of the three national political parties, I was determined to fight it. I helped organize the Canadian Coalition on the Constitution, a group of citizens opposed to the Accord, and I wrote a number of essays that criticized it. Apparently, the premier had read some of these critiques; my most recent one, in the June 1989 issue of *Policy Options*, had prompted him to contact me.

Premier Wells answered the door of the suite himself and invited me in. My first impression was that he was relaxed and informal. This was confirmed during our conversation. Wells is very easy to talk to — not pretentious or glib — and he obviously enjoyed debating the Constitution.

We talked for over an hour about the Meech Lake Accord and other issues. Our points of view were very similar. I was impressed by his sincerity and directness and came away from the meeting feeling decidedly relieved that someone so firmly principled was in a position to stop the Meech Lake Accord.

As I was leaving, Wells mentioned that he needed a constitutional advisor and would be very interested in hiring me. Having just started my employment with the Gordon Foundation in April, I turned down the offer. But we agreed to stay in touch.

After the Quebec election in September, I decided to call Wells to see if he was still determined to rescind Newfoundland's approval of the Accord. He said yes and again offered me the job of constitutional advisor. This time, I decided to consider it seriously. This was Tuesday, September 26. A couple of nights later, the premier called me at home to discuss it again. I had faxed a letter to him the previous day, in which I had said something like, "If you are prepared to rescind Newfoundland's approval of the Accord, I am certainly prepared to come out to Newfoundland and assist you as your constitutional advisor." In his typically scrupulous way, Wells emphasized that he could not in any way "guarantee" that rescission would take place since, among other things, that would be binding the Newfoundland legislature to a certain outcome, which he obviously could not do. I agreed that my employment could not be conditional on rescission. We concluded by setting a time to meet when he came to Toronto the following Wednesday for a speech at Osgoode Hall Law School.

I met Wells about 11 a.m. the following Wednesday at York University. An asbestos alert had just been issued requiring the evacuation of Osgoode Hall, so he and I and his executive assistant, Robert Dornan, went to the main building's cafeteria. I had already decided that I would move to St. John's, and it only took a few moments of conversation to confirm that decision. Wells showed me some of his ideas about changing the Accord, which he had jotted down during his flight to Toronto, and I began to think about exactly what the next step would be.

We were joined briefly by Allan Blakeney, the former premier of Saskatchewan, who had been one of the players during the 1980–81 constitutional talks. He was teaching a course at Osgoode Hall and was responsible for the invitation to Wells to speak to the students that day. Blakeney was a great supporter of the notwithstanding clause — he had opposed the Charter in 1980–81 — and I was encouraged to hear Wells state very forthrightly that the clause simply had to be repealed at the earliest opportunity and that the Charter was an essential instrument of national unity. Needless to say, Blakeney looked uneasy.

I stayed to listen to the premier's speech, which was a punchy critique of the Accord that brought the students to their feet in a standing ovation. Any doubts I might have had about Wells's ability to lead the opposition to Meech were certainly dispelled at this point.

I submitted my letter of resignation to the Gordon Foundation that afternoon. The movers packed me up on Friday and I flew to St. John's on Thanksgiving Sunday. Although I never suspected that the fate of the Accord would remain in the balance until June 23, 1990, I did know that the final and most critical stage of the constitutional debate was beginning.

Early on Tuesday, October 10, I walked in the grey drizzle the short distance from the Holiday Inn to the Confederation Building, where the House of Assembly, Office of the Premier, and other government offices are located. It is an imposing building in bleak surroundings, one mile inland from downtown St. John's and the harbour. It seems to rise out of nowhere and towers above the nearest houses and businesses.

The Office of the Premier is on the eighth floor. I was happy to find that it was modest and unpretentious. Some have called it excessively drab and cramped, but I much preferred it to the more spacious offices in Queen's Park. I had a window facing east, sufficiently angled so that I could see the ocean to the south. The contrast between the concrete jungle in downtown Toronto and the natural, barely inhabited landscape around the Confederation Building could not have been greater.

Before meeting with the premier, I was introduced in a sort of blur to the various employees in the office. I already knew the executive assistant, Robert Dornan, who is young, devoted to the premier, and almost too efficient. Then there were four young special assistants, four secretaries, an office manager, and a receptionist. Judy Foote, a soft-spoken, unflappable woman, was the premier's director of public relations. We soon became friends, in part because we shared the habit of bursting into uncontrollable laughter when confronted with absurd situations.

Edsel Bonnell was Wells's chief of staff. When I first met him, he struck me as cool and gruff as he peered down at me from a significant height. I soon learned that in fact he was one of the warmest and most sensitive people I would ever meet, that he had a great sense of humour, and that he spent much of his spare time co-ordinating and conducting the Gower (United Church) Youth Band, which is highly regarded across Canada. The premier trusted him totally, and no wonder. Edsel is one of those rare types in politics who is direct, no-nonsense, and above political manipulations and conspiracies.

Finally, the premier had two personal secretaries, who were really much more than their titles would suggest. Without them, the office could not have functioned. Margie Stirling, a delightful woman, was the wife of a former leader of the Newfoundland Liberal Party. She had worked with Wells in his law office before he became party leader and was dedicated to him. Her tasks included keeping track of the premier's schedule and organizing his meetings. As the Meech debate heated up, she was sometimes overwhelmed by the number of requests for meetings and by the difficulty of distinguishing between those people who would have to be firmly turned away and those who could be squeezed into his schedule. Margie, who by nature was open and accommodating, found it difficult to turn down more requests than she accepted.

Then there was Rosie Frey — a blur of perpetual energy whose competence in whatever organizational or supervisory task she undertook was intimidating. Yet, like everyone else in the office, she was open, casual, and friendly.

I met with the premier alone later that morning. He welcomed me to the office and we chatted for a while about my flight and the move. As before, he struck me as a good person to work for — open, informal, and fair. After talking for some time, he suggested that my first responsibility might be to draft a letter to the prime minister setting out Newfoundland's concerns with the Meech Lake Accord. I agreed. The premier then showed me some handwritten notes that he had made in May 1987 immediately after the Accord had been announced and while he was campaigning for the Newfoundland Liberal Party leadership. I was impressed by their clarity. Like so many others, he had recognized the implications of the Accord immediately. Virtually all the criticisms that were voiced during the Meech debate were sketched out in those notes, as were many of his ideas for alternative ways to meet Quebec's concerns. From my conversations with Wells and with his staff, I knew that since May 1987 he had been expressing his concerns at every appropriate opportunity. But until he was elected premier in April 1989, he had had no national political weight and had presented no threat to the pro-Meech forces.

I suggested to the premier that I try to draft something structured around Quebec's constitutional demands, and he agreed. I worked on the draft over the next couple of days. This presented a challenge for me, since I was not writing for myself, but for someone who had strong views that were not necessarily identical to mine. Our perspectives were bound to be different. Wells was the premier of a small, have-not province on the edge of "outer Canada," while I was a central Canadian with a "national" point of view. For example, I considered a veto for Quebec to be a necessary means of enhancing that province's sense of security within the Canadian federation; Wells was adamantly opposed to a veto for any province. Wells no doubt believed that vetoes for the large provinces would prevent any constitutional reform that might favour the smaller provinces, particularly in the matter of Senate reform. Other differences between us were substantive. For example, I agreed with the premier that an elected and effective Senate was desirable, but disagreed with him about equal representation for all provinces. He thought it was necessary; I didn't. Despite these differences of opinion, our shared concern to oppose the Accord was sufficient to permit a good working relationship.

I was already aware of the premier's position on the veto and Triple-E Senate and incorporated his views into the first draft of the letter. But another area of disagreement surfaced later when he reviewed my draft comments on the restrictions on the federal spending power. Wells argued that ideally there should be no federal spending in areas of provincial jurisdiction. I believed that this simplistic approach would not wash in today's complex interdependent world and argued that a federal presence was essential in many policy areas to ensure national coherence and minimum national standards.

Yet, as long as poorer provinces like Newfoundland could not afford to discharge their responsibilities adequately, Wells was prepared to acknowledge the value of national shared-cost programs in areas of provincial jurisdiction, particularly if they were aimed at eliminating regional disparity and inequality of opportunities. Although he was strongly critical of the Accord's provisions for federal spending power limitations in the letter to the prime minister, his preference for abolishing the federal spending power never surfaced as a priority in his concerns.

In an attempt to clarify his views for my own sake, I drafted a long, detailed memo to him setting out the arguments in favour of federal intervention in exclusive areas of provincial jurisdiction. The memo came back carefully annotated with question marks and criticisms. Our ensuing discussion was spirited and frustrating. When I realized that I would not be able to change his mind, I decided that I would simply set aside my views for the duration of my employment. This was the first of several intense exchanges that I would have with the premier over the next eight months. While I invariably lost these arguments, my respect for him increased because he was at least prepared to have an open debate on issues and to encourage criticism of his positions.

In drafting the letter, I discovered to my surprise — but also to my relief — that no bureaucrats from the Intergovernmental Affairs Secretariat or the Department of Justice would be involved in the process. I was relieved to find that I was not usurping anyone's role, since there was no one on whom the premier was relying for constitutional advice.

Over the weekend, Wells reworked the first draft of the letter to Mulroney significantly. To my great relief, he left in most of the key points. But in addition to adding some new sections on the Senate and the reform process, he also deleted some sections dealing with the reasons why Quebec did not need special powers — specifically, those which pointed out that Quebec's existing powers were sufficient to preserve and promote the French language and culture. I didn't understand this deletion. I believed it was essential to emphasize this point for those Quebeckers who were convinced that they needed new and special powers to enhance their security. In the months to come, Wells did make passing reference to this point in a few written speeches and letters, but it was never something that would spontaneously enter his mind in interviews and off-the-cuff remarks.

While I was disappointed by that deletion, I was pleased that the premier added a reference describing how Quebec could use its special powers to pass legislation — for example, English-only sign laws — that would set off a *quid pro quo* reaction in the rest of Canada. That reaction would in turn provoke a further reaction in Quebec, until ultimately the French and English retired into two solitudes. This was an eloquent and evocative way of describing the practical, long-term impact of special status.

The letter to Mulroney went through several drafts as the arguments and alternative proposals respecting each of Quebec's five original demands were honed down, together with the premier's criticisms of the process. The premier and I were both careful to ensure that all criticisms were constructive and in no way able to be construed as anti-Quebec. We were genuinely hoping that Quebeckers would be able to analyze the merits of the premier's position and recognize that Newfoundland's opposition to the Accord was both honourable and sincere.

Quebec's five demands were these: recognition of Quebec as a distinct society; recognition of a right of veto over constitutional change; limitations on federal spending power; increased powers over immigration; and participation in the appointment of Supreme Court judges. Wells agreed that Quebec had legitimate concerns in these areas, but disagreed with how they had been accommodated in the Meech Lake Accord. In his view, the Accord not only fatally weakened the federal government — which was disastrous for the poorer, less populous provinces — but also undermined the Canadian Charter and the fundamental equality of citizens of Canada by requiring that the entire Constitution, including the Charter, be interpreted in light of Quebec's role in preserving and promoting its distinct identity.

The final draft of the letter to Mulroney criticized all elements of the Accord, in detail, and offered alternative provisions. For example, it proposed that Supreme Court judges, especially the three civil law judges, be appointed through votes in linguistic divisions in a reformed Senate, such that the civil law judges would require the approval of French-speaking senators. It recommended that the provisions for annual First Ministers' Conferences be deleted, and that the proposed bilateral federal-provincial immigration deals be reconsidered in their entirety. But Wells decided to emphasize his three primary concerns: the creation of a special legislative status for one province; the extension of the requirement for provincial unanimity for constitutional amendments, including now Senate reform; and the provisions relating to limitations on the federal spending power.

Wells also severely criticized the closed-door process that had led to the agreement. In his view, the Accord's merits and demerits had to be openly debated, and each leader had to ensure that his electorate understood the basic issues and had the chance to actively participate in the debate. Wells detested the federal government's insistence that the Accord had to be accepted in spite of the many concerns that were being expressed about it.

In this connection, I came to appreciate that Newfoundlanders and Labradorians are populists by instinct, perhaps because of their relatively recent experience with referenda, and perhaps as well because they seem to be more politically engaged. But the premier's approach to opening up the constitutional reform process was noticed far beyond Newfoundland. It struck a populist chord across Canada. Suddenly the millions of Canadians who had felt excluded and disenfranchised by their political leaders and spokespeople had a representative. Many times in his speeches, I have heard the premier repeat the now-familiar line that he first set out carefully in his original letter to the prime minister: "The worst flaw in the Meech Lake Accord is the process that resulted in the eleven first ministers telling the 26 million people of Canada how they will be governed in the future, instead of the 26 million people of Canada telling the eleven first ministers how they will govern." Whenever the premier made this point in his speeches, it always produced sustained and spontaneous applause.

The letter was finished by the morning of October 18, 1989. The day before, the premier had sent copies to his justice minister, Paul Dicks, and to Dicks's deputy, Jim Thistle. Their comments, when received, did not involve any changes. Edsel Bonnell and Judy Foote also vetted the letter and offered some editorial suggestions, but it essentially reflected the views of the premier.

The letter was sent to the prime minister on the afternoon of October 18, and copies were sent to the other premiers on the same day. None of us had given any clear thought to whether the letter or its contents should be made public. In my view the letter was an excellent summary of and a coherent attack on the Accord's fundamental flaws, and I was impatient for the premier to go on the offensive with it. But the premier viewed it as a private exchange with the prime minister and showed none of my impatience. A First Ministers' Conference was coming up — the first for both the premier and me — and he and I discussed rather inconclusively whether specific legal language should be drafted that could be put forward there to assist discussions on the Accord. Ostensibly, this conference was to focus on the economy, but given the fluid situation, even the bureaucrats could not anticipate what would happen on the constitutional front.

On Friday, October 20, I received an early morning call from Jeffrey Simpson, a *Globe and Mail* journalist, who said that someone in Lowell Murray's office had told him about the premier's letter and that he wanted to write about it. (Murray was the federal minister responsible for federal-provincial relations.) After some discussion, Judy Foote and I concluded that someone would soon leak the letter and — as Simpson had pointed out — the earlier it came out the better if we wanted to bring it to public attention. If we waited until the following week, it would be lost in the fallout created by the Manitoba and New Brunswick reports on Meech, which were due for release on October 23 and 24 respectively.

Judy and I favoured releasing the letter as soon as possible, but knew the premier might resist. His impeccable though sometimes infuriating sense of fair play had led him to insist that the prime minister be given a reasonable chance to respond, and Mulroney was out of the country. By noon, we had drafted a press release that set out the contents of the letter, with only the personal elements edited out.

Judy and I met with the premier in the early afternoon. We told him about Simpson's call, and Judy gave her opinion that the contents of the letter should be released officially as soon as possible so that the premier could control the situation. The alternative was to wait until someone leaked the letter, in which event he might have to react in a disorganized, ineffective way. As expected, the premier preferred to let the prime minister respond first and was not convinced that a leak was inevitable. He also was adamant about not wanting the media to force events and did not see the importance of being ahead of the Manitoba and New Brunswick reports.

When it became obvious that we were at an impasse, the premier called in Edsel Bonnell for his advice. I was apprehensive, since I did not yet know Edsel very well and believed that he would probably agree with the premier. But after listening intently to the arguments, Edsel tipped the scales in favour of release, noting that it couldn't really be an affront to the federal government since it was Lowell Murray's office itself that was responsible for the preliminary leak to Simpson. The premier gave the go-ahead.

Minutes later, Judy and I were sitting next to fax machines, transmitting the release to the media, ultimately until almost midnight. In retrospect, the timing was perfect. The release received major front-page coverage the next day, which ensured that the position of Newfoundland and Labrador was well-known days before the positions of Manitoba and New Brunswick were made clear. This was to be the first of many examples of our "non-strategy" over the ensuing eight to nine months. Fortunately, this decision worked out well.

After tracking the response to the premier's letter in the media over the weekend, I returned to the office on Monday, anticipating the Manitoba government's report on Meech. Both the premier and I were already aware of the broad outlines of the report through phone calls from Sharon Carstairs, the leader of the Liberals in Manitoba. At this point, Carstairs was staunchly anti-Meech, having declared "Meech is dead" after her surprising win as opposition leader in the provincial election. She obviously saw an ally in Wells and probably felt that it would be valuable to give him some advance warning of what was likely to be in Manitoba's report. She must have also known that the report was going to be significantly watered down for the sake of achieving consensus among Manitoba's three provincial parties, and that Wells would be freer than her to pursue more principled opposition to the Accord.

When the report was finally delivered by courier to the Office of the Premier around 3 p.m. on October 23, I read it immediately. A quick look confirmed my fears. While it recommended some major amendments, it basically attempted to "fix" the Accord by either dropping provisions or adding on new subsections and some rather contorted qualifications.

Wells was in Ottawa that day and not due to arrive back by plane until about 10 p.m. Since requests for his reaction were already flowing in and would have to be met very early the next morning, my only opportunity to meet with him to discuss the report would be at the airport and during the drive down to his house. I worked until 9:30 that night and then took a taxi from the office to meet his flight.

The premier had been told to expect me. He was tired but was interested in talking about the report, however briefly. This was my first experience with briefing him on a specific document. What I discovered was that he did not want to be bothered with the petty details of the report's recommendations. Instead he zoomed in on the area of particular interest to him — the recommendations on the distinct society clause.

He had already heard through the media that day that Manitoba had recommended that the role of the Quebec government and legislature should be to "uphold" rather than "preserve and promote" Quebec's distinct society. Wells's immediate reaction during the drive to his home was that this change did not eliminate the creation of a special legislative status for Quebec. He seemed to feel that he needed only to deal with this one point when responding in the media to Manitoba's report, that he didn't need to discuss all the details of the changes to the distinct society clause. Of course, he was right, since most of his interviews would involve thirty-second television clips, and print journalists would summarize his reaction in one or two lines at most.

During the drive we had time to discuss a few other points, such as the recommendation to drop the proposal for a limitation on the federal spending power. Carstairs had already relayed this point a few days earlier. Apparently Manitoba's task force simply could not reconcile the views of the Manitoba Liberals and NDP (who wanted loose restrictions) with those of the Tories (who wanted to strengthen them); the three parties, for the sake of consensus, had recommended deleting the proposal. Wells considered this regrettable and thought that at least Newfoundland was being constructive in proposing adjustments or amendments to the proposal.

After talking with the premier, I felt that I ought to set out the details of the Manitoba report more carefully. So I stayed up late writing a more detailed memo for him to study in the morning. I recognized that the premier's public statements needed only to focus on one or two elements, but I thought he ought to at least be aware of the details. And I knew that he would always take the time to read even a long memo, especially when it dealt with the constitutional debate.

The strength of the report was that it recommended major amendments to the Accord; these, if pursued, would inevitably require that the Accord be reopened. For example, it recommended that the distinct society clause be broadened to become a "Canada clause" that recognized, among other things, the existence of Canada as a federal state with a distinct national identity. I also welcomed the task force's conclusion that any reference to Quebec's distinct society would have to be balanced by a reference to other fundamental characteristics of Canada so that the true nature of Canada's national identity was more accurately reflected. These fundamental characteristics were to include the existence of the aboriginal peoples as a distinct and fundamental part of Canada, and the existence of Canada's multicultural heritage. Manitoba's ongoing insistence on some form of Canada clause was to have a major impact on the remainder of the Meech debate.

The weakness of the Manitoba report was that it failed to provide a coherent alternative to the Accord. Instead, it confined itself to contorted amendments. Admittedly, the report was the product of open public hearings examining only the Accord itself and no other alternative, and it had to satisfy all three parties in a minority government. But the inevitable result was that it made some disconnected recommendations that, apart from the Canada clause proposal, offered no clear alternative vision of the country. For example, in an area such as powers over immigration, the report outlined all the valid concerns over the disintegration of essential federal powers, but then it fizzled out with a recommendation for a future review of the operation of the Meech provisions.

Similarly, the report made no recommendation for change on the proposal to allow all provinces to opt out, with compensation, of any constitutional amendment transferring legislative power to the federal government. The reason, ostensibly, was that none of the presentations made to the task force had raised any real concerns. Most experts agreed, however, that this change to the general amending formula was as significant as the extension of the veto in other areas. It virtually guaranteed that there could never be another amendment like the critical one in 1940 that gave the federal government jurisdiction over unemployment insurance. In fact, the opting-out clause was the equivalent of giving Quebec — and indeed, all provinces — a complete veto over all amendments. This was acknowledged by Quebec politicians of every political stripe. More specifically, although a province could not stop an undesirable amendment, up to three provinces having 50 percent of the population could simply declare that it did not apply and, having done so, receive compensation from the federal government. I was constantly angered by the federal government's deliberate obfuscation of the real impact of this change and regretted that Manitoba's task force had been unable to challenge the pro-Meech orthodoxy on this issue.

The next morning, the premier gave a number of interviews to print journalists and radio and television reporters. I was impressed by how smoothly and efficiently Judy was able to arrange the premier's time and cram in the maximum number of interviews, both in his office and at the nearby CBC studio. I was equally impressed with the premier's resilience. He clearly thrived on public debate; he never seemed to tire of answering the same questions from different reporters, but remained courteous and articulate throughout.

While the premier was giving interviews on the Manitoba report, New Brunswick's report was being released. For some reason, our copy from Premier Frank McKenna's office did not arrive until the following day, so I had to scramble to have a friend at the University of New Brunswick fax the report to us. He warned me that the report basically left the Accord intact and that McKenna by now had completely capitulated. He was right. New Brunswick's report expressed some mild concerns with the Accord, but concluded either that they did not justify reopening the Accord or that they could be dealt with by way of amendments. For example, with respect to the impact on the Charter, it acknowledged that the vast majority of the presentations called for a clear statement that the Charter would be paramount over the "distinct society" and "fundamental characteristics" clauses. Yet it then concluded as follows: "To make the Charter paramount in all circumstances would in effect render the entrenchment of section 2 of the Accord meaningless. Because of this, the Committee cannot accept the recommendation dealing with the paramountcy of the Charter."

As I noted in an irreverent memo to the premier — one of the 400 I would write in the coming months — Gil Rémillard or Lowell Murray could not have said it any better. It was truly astounding as so many callers to Wells's office that day angrily pointed out, that the New Brunswick report could conclude that the Charter was undermined and yet not recommend that something be done about it. Already Wells was being viewed as the last real hope for Meech opponents.

Later in the afternoon, I had a chance to speak to the premier about the New Brunswick report. Again, he was primarily interested at this point in how it dealt with such key issues as the distinct society clause. He seemed disappointed rather than surprised by the report; he had been aware of the rumours that McKenna's opposition to the Accord had been weakening, and the report simply confirmed those rumours. It seemed to me that Wells was fully aware of how different he and McKenna were in how they approached Meech. McKenna, for example, had never been as clearly opposed to the Accord as the premier.

Why McKenna gradually abandoned his opposition after raising the expectations of the general public so high is difficult to understand. My instinctive conclusion, which was increasingly fortified in the ensuing months, was that McKenna's shift and New Brunswick's report were the result of some very intense activity in the Fredericton-Quebec City-Toronto-Ottawa quadrangle. In my judgment, the feds, David Peterson, and Robert Bourassa immediately recognized the threat that McKenna presented to the Accord after his election as premier in the fall of 1987 and decided to do something about it. In addition, Peterson certainly appreciated that there was intense opposition to the Accord in Ontario, as well as widespread discontent with the findings of his own constitutional committee, which in mid-1988 had recommended that the Accord be approved as it stood, with any remaining concerns to be dealt with in future rounds and additional accords. Bourassa's desire to see Meech passed intact was not surprising, given his close relationship with Mulroney and his recognition that, under Meech, Quebec had achieved a special status that could be expanded in future discussions. Peterson's co-operation with Mulroney was less easy to understand. In my view, Peterson realized that he had missed his chance to play statesman and principled politician back at the Langevin Block meeting in June 1987, when he could have stopped the Accord at its inception. But having caved in to pressure from Bourassa and Mulroney, he and his close associates (like his attorney general,

Ian Scott) became almost evangelical in trying to justify their support for the Accord.

Scuttlebutt suggests that Peterson was instrumental in bringing McKenna into line. (The Ontario Liberals helped McKenna a great deal during his election.) Perhaps Peterson suggested that McKenna could play an important role in nation-building by persuading the opposition forces to support amendments or add-ons to the Accord that would not challenge the fundamental reforms. It is also likely that many pro-Meechers — for example, Lowell Murray — believed that McKenna was in a good position to soften the opposition, being the popular and trusted premier of an officially bilingual province. At the same time, Peterson had a close rapport with Bourassa and was regarded by Ottawa as a good go-between for the save-the-Accord operations.

Unlike Clyde Wells, Frank McKenna does not appear to have, or at least cannot articulate, a consistent vision of the Canadian nation. As a politician, he certainly listened to his province's various interest groups — women's groups, aboriginal groups, francophone groups, and so on. But he was ultimately snared by the insiders in Ottawa, Toronto, and Quebec City, whose approach to constitution-making was both élitist and lacking in principle. As a result, he was unable to take the populist approach to constitution making, which requires a broad vision and approaches constitutions as immutable documents whose main purpose is to articulate principles and values.

Yet another part of the explanation for New Brunswick's position had to do with McKenna's advisors. Francis McGuire, one of his closest aides, was a former assistant to Liberal MP Raymond Garneau. McGuire must have been influenced to some extent by Garneau's view of the Accord. Garneau had lost the leadership of the Quebec Liberal Party to Bourassa and then run for the federal Liberals in 1984. He was Liberal leader John Turner's Quebec lieutenant during the negotiations that led to the Accord. He resigned soon afterwards and is now a prominent Quebec businessman. He strongly supported distinct society status for Quebec and was of the school that simply wanted the constitutional issue settled as quickly as possible, so that the country could get on with other things. His world, like that of most Quebec business leaders, seemed to revolve around Quebec.

In addition, as I was to discover a little later, the same bureaucrats who had helped Richard Hatfield to negotiate the Accord were also advising and negotiating for McKenna. These included the deputy minister of intergovernmental affairs, Don Dennison, and the justice department's constitutional advisor, Bruce Juda. They must have had some vested interest in the Accord as it stood, or at the very least some difficulty in changing their frames of reference to contemplate reopening rather than just amending it.

So there existed a large cadre of career bureaucrats who had helped to draft and defend the Accord and who typically had a good deal of influence over their first ministers. This factor, which was not visible to the public, was also present in Newfoundland. In St. John's, the key bureaucrats in both the Intergovernmental Affairs Secretariat and the Department of Justice had all worked with the previous Conservative government under Brian Peckford and had advised him on the Meech Lake Accord. When the premier decided to seek out a constitutional advisor, he did so primarily because there was no one in the bureaucracy who had the legal and public policy background to work closely with him and articulate his ideas. I learned shortly after my arrival that the deputy minister of justice, Jim Thistle, also disagreed with the premier's legal interpretation of the distinct society clause. The premier, although he respected Thistle's views, was unswayed by them: as a constitutional lawyer himself, he had faith in his own conclusions.

I had been brought in as a bureaucrat — technically, I reported to the deputy minister of intergovernmental affairs. Yet because I was located in the premier's office, I had virtually no contact with the secretariat. One result was that the Tory opposition alleged during Question Period that I was a "Dalton Camp" and criticized the premier's decision to hire a non-Newfoundlander. (Mulroney at one point had hired Camp, a long-time Conservative, to work in the Privy Council Office. The opposition had alleged that he was really a political appointee and should have been paid as a member of the political staff.)

Because the Meech debate was more or less self-contained and unconnected to other intergovernmental issues, in effect I worked around the bureaucrats. But this independence also meant that there were no Newfoundland bureaucrats "in the loop" on the Meech issue. As I was to find a few weeks later at the November First Ministers' Conference, there has developed across Canada a fairly cosy relationship among intergovernmental officials in all provincial capitals. Someone like me, who was not connected and who held strong views on the Accord — unlike most bureaucrats — did not easily fit in. Another, more important effect of the premier's hands-on approach to the Accord was that it totally disrupted bureaucratic lines of communication and left the other first ministers and bureaucrats at a loss about how to deal with the premier.

The premier and I never directly discussed "staying out of the loop" until a later stage of the debate. Until Ottawa and the other pro-Meech provinces showed some flexibility on Newfoundland's concerns, the premier saw little reason for me to contact my counterparts, except to exchange information.

One thing that astounded me was the almost total lack of contact between the premier's office and the Federal-Provincial Relations Office in Ottawa. Normally, in a well-functioning federation, you would expect the FPRO to be actively in contact with *all* provincial officials, whatever their position. In this case, with a constitutional impasse looming, official Ottawa seemed unable to deal with Newfoundland. To my knowledge, the FPRO only once communicated directly with us; that was in May 1990, when they faxed to the premier's office a copy of Roger Tassé's brief to the Charest Committee.

My only direct talks at the bureaucratic level were with the two New Brunswick officials, Don Dennison and Bruce Juda. On February 8, 1990, we met to discuss New Brunswick's forthcoming initiative for a parallel accord. This occasion was doubly unusual in that I also met with key officials from the Newfoundland Intergovernmental Affairs Secretariat. In late March I had a further conversation with the New Brunswick Intergovernmental Affairs deputy minister to discuss the actual details of the parallel accord. In my view, on both occasions, New Brunswick officials were acting as Ottawa's proxies in an attempt to open up the lines to St. John's, and there is no doubt that within minutes of my conversation in late March, in which I criticized most of the proposed New Brunswick add-ons, the information had been conveyed to the FPRO.

The impact of my not being "in the loop" was obvious at the February meeting, where the New Brunswick officials suggested that since there was some movement toward a parallel accord, "wouldn't it be better to be in on designing the package?" I had no hesitation in saying no. On this occasion I discussed my isolation with the premier, and he supported my conclusion that Newfoundland should not participate in the New Brunswick initiative. It was the first and last attempt, at the officials' level, to co-opt Newfoundland in the matter of a "parallel accord."

As my first few weeks in the premier's office drew to a close, it was clear that the Meech debate had entered a new phase. With Wells's letter to the prime minister and the Manitoba and New Brunswick reports, Ottawa was finally waking up to the opposition and to Wells as its most articulate spokesman.

TWO

The Newfoundland
Alternative Accord

S EVERAL DAYS AFTER Wells's letter to Mulroney was released to the public, the premier raised the idea of taking specific constitutional amendments to the upcoming November First Ministers' Conference. The purpose would be to translate into concrete amendments the more general changes set out in Wells's letter to the prime minister.

I was mildly opposed to the idea. My personal view was that specific amendments in "legalese" might confuse the debate on the more general criticisms set out in the premier's letter. At the same time, I saw some merit in demonstrating that the premier was ready, willing, and able to enter immediately into constructive negotiations to amend the Accord.

The formulation of the amendments was a technical exercise requiring considerable legal skill. Given my "diluted" status as a lawyer — I had only practised law for one year six years before — I warned the premier that my attempted draft would be less than adequate. I did not have to worry — the premier was an experienced and skilled legal draftsman. He obviously enjoyed annotating and rewriting my drafts, and I sometimes wondered whether I was contributing anything at all. He knew precisely what he wanted to get across, and I was amazed at how quickly he could shift his focus from whatever he was doing to provide an immediate comment on a particular section. This attention to minute legal detail was to be my only real concern with the premier over the next few months.

He was sometimes too much the lawyer, and not enough the politician.

During the drafting of the alternative accord, I became used to him suddenly appearing at the door of my office en route to a cabinet meeting or the House of Assembly. He would stop by to bring in an annotated draft with further suggestions for change and would often make some joke about the twelve filing cabinets stuffed into my office, the expanding number of bulletin boards on my walls — all of them covered with Meech cartoons — and the mountains of paper piled on any available space, including the floor. His easy-going approach always impressed me.

When we were finalizing the document on November 4–5, which was the weekend before the First Ministers' Conference, we discussed what to call it. Ultimately, the premier settled on an "Alternative to the Meech Lake Accord." He and I had both watched a CBC Newsworld interview with Lowell Murray that Sunday morning. In his typically cool, expressionless, inscrutable manner, Murray asserted that while Manitoba, New Brunswick, and "Premier Wells"* had criticized the Accord, it was to no avail since no one had produced an alternative that could attract unanimity the way Meech Lake had. Of course, neither the premier nor I thought for a moment that the Newfoundland alternative would provide the magic answer and attract the unanimity Murray spoke of, but at least by putting forward a concrete alternative, the premier was following up his criticisms with a constructive initiative. His proposals should have become the subject of widespread debate, counter-proposals, amendments, and so forth. But these were not ordinary circumstances, and the pro-Meech forces were going to make sure it didn't happen that way.

The premier decided that the alternative accord should track the contents of his letter to the prime minister fairly closely; that is, it should address each of Quebec's five demands in turn and in most cases provide alternative ways to accommodate them in the Constitution. In his letter to the prime minister, the premier had suggested that Quebec's distinctiveness be recognized in the preamble to the Constitution rather than in the distinct society clause. The recognition would then have only symbolic value and would not create a

* Murray and the feds were constantly trying to marginalize the premier and argue that he was a one-man show without the support of the legislature.

special legislative status for Quebec or allow the Quebec government to override the Charter. The premier decided that an entirely new preamble should be drafted and suggested that the distinct society clause be recast as a preamble. I then suggested that the remainder of the preamble could state the fundamental characteristics set out in Manitoba's proposal for a Canada clause. I thought this would be a good way to link Newfoundland with its closest ally. But the premier would always prefer the preamble approach over Manitoba's proposal that the distinct society clause be converted into a Canada clause. In part, this was because a preamble made no reference to the roles and responsibilities of governments, and could not be used to override the Charter.

Of course, the premier was under no illusions as to how Quebec would react. From my perspective, one could only hope that this proposal would at least open the long-suppressed debate about how Quebec is already preserving and promoting its distinctiveness using its existing powers. In addition, to the extent that the courts already take into account Quebec's distinctiveness in Charter cases by virtue of section 1 of the Charter, which deals with reasonable limits, the preamble reference would be a reinforcing factor.

The second element of Newfoundland's alternative accord had to do with a veto for Quebec over constitutional changes affecting language, culture, and the appointment of civil law judges. In Wells's proposal, this veto would be exercised through Quebec senators at the national level. This is where the premier began to develop his theory of "the three equalities" — equality of citizens in the House of Commons, equality of provinces in a reformed Senate, and equality of the French and English linguistic cultures. Although he remained adamant that no provincial government should have a veto over constitutional change, he argued that the third equality did justify a limited veto for Quebec — but operating through a *national* institution, the Senate, rather than a provincial government.

The premier's concept of the three equalities was intellectually vigorous and obviously well thought out. He explained to me that he began to develop this idea in the 1970s, when he was helping to draft the Canadian Bar Association's report on the Constitution. At that time, he had supported the creation of a third house of Parliament — in addition to the House of

Commons and the Senate — through which the third equality could be expressed. He had since concluded that it would create a totally unwieldy government structure. A limited veto for francophone senators through special votes in the Senate was much more practicable.

The third element of Newfoundland's alternative had to do with ensuring that the restrictions on the federal spending power were consistent with the obligations in the Constitution Act, 1982. These obligations included the following: promotion of equal opportunities among Canadians and the provision of essential public services of reasonable quality to all Canadians. The premier himself drafted what was in effect an "add-on" to the Meech proposal; it stated that the restrictions would not apply when Parliament expressly declared that federal spending was for these purposes. He was convinced that Quebec, and other proponents of the idea that the federal spending power should be limited, would not object to this.

My personal view was that he was expecting too much — that the other premiers were going to interpret his proposal as a licence for Parliament to get around any restrictions whenever it liked simply by making a declaration. Yet I didn't particularly mind such an interpretation since I was much more concerned than the premier about the preservation of the federal spending power and the establishment of minimum national standards. The premier's main concern was to ensure targeted federal spending; for example, spending for specific public services in the poorer provinces. The goal was to bring those services up to the standards of the richer provinces — in effect, to allow the richer provinces to establish the standards. In my view, however, the federal government has a critical independent role in this matter, which is to use its spending power and shared-cost programs to establish minimum standards for all provinces — including the richer ones, since one cannot always guarantee that the richer ones will pursue the appropriate standards. Our differences in this area remained throughout the debate, but after conceding defeat, I provided as much support as I could for the premier's proposals.

The fourth element of Newfoundland's alternative was the proposal that the appointments to the Supreme Court of Canada be subject to approval by the Senate. Again, the premier himself drafted the specific provisions; like the mechanism for constitutional amendments, they involved separate consideration by French and English divisions of the Senate to ensure that Quebec senators would have the last word on civil law appointments.

The fifth element addressed the immigration provisions in the Accord, which as they now stood effectively emasculated the federal role in immigration. The premier and I could not arrive at any satisfactory alternatives or amendments and simply suggested that the provisions had to be completely rethought.

Finally, Newfoundland's alternative recommended deleting the provisions for entrenched First Ministers' Conferences. The premier felt that these would inevitably lead to a third unaccountable level of government and further undermine the coherence and strength of the national government. Since 1987 he had ridiculed the supposed victory of his predecessor, Brian Peckford, in having included a mandatory annual discussion of fisheries' roles and responsibilities. He argued that Newfoundland did not need more constitutional jurisdiction over fisheries, and that an annual first ministers' discussion would likely not lead to anything concrete anyway.

The premier also decided that he wanted to append an actual amendment for a Triple-E Senate. I was able to find such a draft in a publication of the Canada West Foundation, and the premier himself adapted it. Again, he hoped to kickstart the debate and demonstrate his willingness to negotiate in earnest.

The document went through several drafts, and the premier discussed it at least twice with his cabinet. To the best of my recollection — I did not, of course, attend the cabinet meetings — only a couple of more or less technical changes were suggested by the other ministers. The premier unquestionably had the support of his government for the alternative accord.

During this period, I prepared some briefing notes for the Liberal Party. These outlined the constitutional background and the details of Newfoundland's position, particularly as set out in the letter to the prime minister. I was also invited to a caucus meeting one morning to answer questions. The premier encouraged my participation since he wanted to ensure that the caucus understood and supported the position we had outlined.

A couple of weeks after the public release of Wells's letter to Mulroney, the prime minister responded. About mid-morning on November 2, Rosie Frey buzzed me on the telephone and asked me to come to the premier's office immediately. Mulroney had just called. Edsel Bonnell, Robert Dornan, and I stayed in the office during the conversation. While we could not hear Mulroney's words since there was no speaker phone, we could get a good idea of what he was saying from the premier's replies.

As usual, the premier was courteous. Apparently Mulroney started out by mentioning that he had seen Wells's daughter Heidi, who was a bilingual law student in Moncton, New Brunswick, being interviewed on a news program. For me, this was classic Mulroney — he was always looking for some personal element with which to turn on the charm. The premier acknowledged the pleasantries, but he quickly turned their conversation to a direct exchange of positions on the Accord.

For about a quarter of an hour, the prime minister went through the standard pro-Meech arguments. (A few hours later a long letter setting these out arrived by fax.) The premier was polite but firm in stating his fundamental disagreement with the Accord. From time to time, he was also exasperated. A few points stand out. First, the premier clearly rebutted Mulroney's arguments that Quebec was excluded when the Constitution was patriated in 1982. He told the prime minister firmly that he was wrong and said that Ottawa had every right to act as it did, since the majority of federal MPs, including those from Quebec, had supported the patriation and that in any event no one province should be able to hold up our constitutional development.

The prime minister then raised the issue of the notwithstanding clause, which states that Parliament or the legislature of a province can declare that certain legislation shall operate notwithstanding a breach of certain fundamental freedoms, and legal and equality rights, for a renewable period of five years. Mulroney said that in Quebec the clause was regarded as essential, in that it protected that province's interests against federal encroachment. This position of course is a regurgitation of the Quebec nationalist line and a misunderstanding of the nature of an entrenched Charter of Rights and Freedoms. The premier politely indicated that the prime minister's view of the Charter and the notwithstanding clause was incorrect — the Charter gave the Canadian people rights and freedoms to be asserted against all governments, while the notwithstanding clause gave governments certain limited scope to override those rights and freedoms. Thus, the use of the notwithstanding clause was a question not of one government versus another, but of a government versus the people. The premier also put on the record his support for the repeal of the notwithstanding clause at the earliest opportunity.

As I listened to Wells's end of this conversation, I realized that I was witnessing yet another example of the prime minister's insensitivity to the populist aspect of constitutional reform and of his fixation with executive-style intergovernmental relations. If he could not understand how the Charter operated and was consumed with the government's perspective rather than the concerns of individuals, then he was insensitive to the very basis of a modern liberal democracy — not a very reassuring conclusion. Given Mulroney's previously expressed public concern with the very existence of the notwithstanding clause (a few months earlier he had irresponsibly stated that the clause made the Constitution not worth the paper it is written on), the entire discussion further confirmed my impression that the prime minister was not operating according to any firm sense of constitutional principles.

Finally, the prime minister argued that the premier's fundamental precept of the equality of provinces justified giving the veto to all provinces. Mulroney also suggested less than subtly that the premier was at odds with Jean Chrétien, who supported a full veto for Quebec on all constitutional change. This was one more example of Mulroney's frequent attempts to use the debate over the Accord to encourage splits among Liberals for purely partisan advantage. The premier declined the bait and politely corrected the prime minister's misinterpretation: the equality of the provinces related to the exercise of legislative power vis-à-vis the federal government and to representation in the Senate. The constitutional amending formula was outside this: it related to changing the fundamental law of the nation and required a different approach.

Throughout the debate over the Meech Lake Accord, the premier's opposition to any extension of the constitutional veto to any province was constantly misinterpreted by many pro-Meech forces; deliberately and deceptively, they suggested that he was anti-Quebec and that he was opposed to a veto because he wanted Senate reform to be forced on Quebec. On the contrary, he never suggested that changes as significant as

Senate reform would occur without Quebec's consent. But the fact that no single province had a veto would clearly result in a more flexible negotiating atmosphere, particularly for smaller provinces.

After Mulroney hung up, the premier had to return to a meeting that he had interrupted, but he quickly gave us the highlights of Mulroney's side of the conversation. Later that same afternoon, a long letter from the prime minister arrived by fax. Its contents were predictable and frustrating, while its tone was condescending. It spent some four pages out of a total of fourteen setting out Canada's constitutional history à la Brian Mulroney and alleging that the Meech proposals were simply the logical conclusion of twenty years of discussion. As the premier often stated, anyone who is the least bit familiar with the unequivocal federal opposition to special status for Quebec up to 1984 would have to conclude that Mulroney's account could not have been further from the truth. The remainder of Mulroney's letter followed the structure of the premier's letter and responded to the premier's arguments with respect to each of Quebec's demands.

I was not at first convinced that a reply to Mulroney's letter was necessary, since the disagreements between Wells and the prime minister were so fundamental. But if a reply was necessary, I preferred a frontal attack on all of the many points it raised. A couple of days later, the premier himself dictated a reasonably short letter that focused on three or four particularly egregious points, such as Mulroney's rewriting of history. For the most part, I only did some editing.

In one area, however, I strongly disagreed with the premier. This concerned his statement that if the prime minister sincerely believed that the distinct society clause would not create additional legislative jurisdiction for Quebec, then he should not object to a new subsection that would read, "Nothing in subsection 3 grants any power to the legislature and government of Quebec in excess of the power of the legislature and government of any other province." I believed that such an amendment was exactly the type of add-on that federal officials would play with in an attempt to "save" and "add to" the Accord. And while it might limit the scope of the distinct society clause, it would definitely not lessen the damage to the Charter. In addition, whatever the legal merits, the premier would leave himself open to accusations from Charter activists that he was not really concerned with the impact of roles and responsibilities of governments on our Charter rights, just as long as Newfoundland had the same rights as the Quebec government.

I made these arguments to the premier and suggested that, if necessary, he just reiterate his proposal to recognize Quebec's distinctiveness in a new preamble. The premier rejected my arguments, although in the end he agreed to insert a qualifying sentence that read, "There is however a better way to provide for the constitutional accommodation of Quebec's distinct society" — a reference to the preamble proposal.

Charter rights was one area in which I would continue to have disagreements with the premier. Although he was certainly supportive of individual rights and freedoms as entrenched in the Charter, he was not instinctive about how the Charter operates to insulate individual rights from certain actions by government. Rather, he was much more instinctive about the exercise of legislative powers and the structure of government. For example, when he referred to "equality of citizens" — his "first equality" — he usually meant the equality of representation of citizens in the House of Commons (that is, one person, one vote). Indeed, when he was first drafting his description of the fundamental precepts of federalism and the three equalities, one of which was the equality of citizens, he initially left out any reference to the Charter. Of course he easily agreed to its insertion, but it always struck him as somewhat incidental.

In contrast, for me and many other observers, "equality of citizens" referred to the equal application of Charter rights to all Canadians so that we all asserted the same rights against all our governments, whether federal or provincial. Among other things, this means that no government should be given the enhanced power to justify limits on our fundamental rights. The distinct society clause would offer exactly that, and the fact that this power might be extended equally to all provincial governments was reprehensible. Unfortunately, at times the premier's main concern was to ensure that there was no special legislative status for one province. As a result, he was sometimes insensitive to the Charter aspect.

The final internal debate that took place in the premier's office before the First Ministers' Conference of November 9–10 was on the issue of the rescission of the previous government's approval of the Accord. In July 1988 the Conservative government of Brian Peckford had approved the Accord. That government had never held public hearings before approving it and indeed had blocked any coherent legislative debate on it. I knew that the premier was confident that he had the mandate to rescind the Peckford government's approval if satisfactory changes were not made. He had been making his position very clear since his election as party leader in June 1987, and he had discussed it at every opportunity in interviews with the national media during his election campaign in the spring of 1989, although the provincial Tories declined to make the Accord a specific election issue. The general consensus was that he had been as fair and forthright as possible with the people of Newfoundland and Labrador and would be justified in eventually seeking rescission.

I felt strongly that the sooner the rescission took place, the better — that it would convince the other first ministers of the premier's determination and force a debate on the Accord's future well before the June 23 deadline. The speculation in the press once again was veering away from substance and toward procedural and tactical issues like the rescission. I believed that early rescission could bring the debate back to substance.

The premier was aware of my position. From others, he heard some complex proposals to table a motion to rescind and use it as a lever to make certain changes to the Accord. At every opportunity I commented unfavourably on such proposals, and I was reassured to find that the premier agreed. The government would either rescind or not — there would be no Machiavellian manipulations of a rescission motion. I also knew that rescission was not on the premier's immediate agenda and did not bother to continually reiterate my already well-known view.

I found, however, that Judy Foote also believed that the sooner rescission took place the better. A couple of days before the November conference, we met with the premier and argued for immediate rescission. The premier listened closely but remained adamant that rescission, or even the introduction of a motion to rescind, would be a provocative act just before the First Ministers' Conference. No doubt Ontario's David Peterson and others had expressed this view to him, since it is precisely the message that was given to me on the eve of the conference by Patrick Monahan, a key policy advisor in Peterson's office.

Monahan and I had known each other from law school in the late 1970s. At first, I was surprised by his strong and vocal support for the Accord, given my recollection of his views during the debate leading up to the 1980 referendum. I assumed he was merely being loyal to his employers — first to Ontario's attorney general, Ian Scott, and later to David Peterson. Yet as time went by, and it became clear that his *modus operandi* emphasized process over substance, I concluded he was consumed with the political game of saving Meech intact.

His call to me was definitely of the "nudge-nudge" variety. I suppose he hoped that he could establish a back-door influence on Wells. I was decidedly cool and emphasized that regardless of timing, rescission was inevitable at some point, if only to implement the changes required to satisfy Newfoundland's concerns. Our contacts after this were chilly.

Undoubtedly, any move to rescind the Accord prior to the First Ministers' Conference would have had an electric impact. At the same time, any delay was going to play into the hands of the Federal-Provincial Relations Office and the equivalent Ontario unit. A key mandate of both groups was to save Meech and isolate Newfoundland. Because I was all too conscious of my limitations as a strategist, I was grateful to Edsel Bonnell for intermittently warning the premier that Mulroney operated according to pure political calculations and not principle and that he should be wary of sandbags. The premier's openness and his willingness to look for the best in people and to believe the best has always impressed me. Certainly, these aspects of his character are refreshing in this period of cynical politics.

The premier tabled Newfoundland's alternative accord in the House of Assembly on November 8, the day before the First Ministers' Conference, and was given a full hour of Newsworld coverage for the subsequent press conference. At this point I began to appreciate the far-reaching impact of the all-news channel on Canadian politics. Again and again, we discovered that this channel was probably the single most effective way of reaching the Canadian public from coast to coast. It contributed greatly to the groundswell of popular support that was starting to build for Premier Wells.

With the tabling of the alternative accord, it seemed to me that the momentum was definitely on the side of the Meech opposition. After all the intense drafting and redrafting of documents, there was now a slight lull as we all waited to see how the other first ministers would respond at the forthcoming conference.

THREE

The First Ministers'
Conference on the Economy

I N THE VERY EARLY MORNING on Wednesday, November 8, I joined the premier, Mrs. Wells, Judy Foote, Robert Dornan, and Rosie Frey at the airport for the flight to the First Ministers' Conference in Ottawa. Joining us there would be two assistant deputy ministers of intergovernmental affairs, Barbara Knight and Fred Way; the cabinet secretary, Hal Stanley; the finance minister, Hubert Kitchen; and the justice minister, Paul Dicks.

I was anticipating the conference with curiosity, particularly the reaction to Wells's letter to the prime minister. Of course, the conference was ostensibly about the economy. But we all knew that it would inevitably focus on the Constitution, since it was coming so soon after the Manitoba and New Brunswick reports on the Accord and Wells's letter to the prime minister.

We were staying at the Westin Hotel in downtown Ottawa, right across from the Conference Centre where the formal meetings on Thursday and Friday were to be held. The first event, however, was a dinner of the first ministers that evening at the new National Art Gallery.

During the afternoon, Wells completed the text of his opening statement. The first draft had been prepared by the Intergovernmental Affairs Secretariat and focused mainly on economic issues — the fisheries crisis and the environment. I had contributed a large chunk on the constitutional issues, which the premier trimmed down significantly. Even so, I thought it was clear and punchy enough to attract some attention.

The premier, Judy, Barbara Knight and I headed over in a car to the art gallery shortly before 6 p.m. Barbara and I were attending the parallel "officials" dinner, and of course Judy was indispensable, since the premier was mobbed by the media at every opportunity. Sure enough, as we emerged from the car, we were blinded by the television lights. Dozens of journalists were pressing against barrier gates, shouting questions at Wells at the same time. Most of their questions were about rescission, and I was pleased to hear the premier say, more or less, that it would have to take place at some point.

The premier headed into the private dining room, while Barbara and I joined the bureaucrats from the other provinces and the federal government. I recognized a few people, such as Patrick Monahan from Ontario, but for the most part I had to rely on Barbara for introductions. She had been working with Newfoundland's Intergovernmental Affairs Secretariat for at least a decade and knew most of the other provincial representatives. The atmosphere was friendly, like some sort of school reunion. Everyone with whom we spoke studiously avoided any discussion of Meech. They seemed uncomfortable about the possibility that Newfoundland might kill the Accord or contemplate major changes to it.

The premiers and prime minister emerged around 10 p.m. Wells looked exhausted. Apparently he had had some heated arguments with the prime minister and several of the premiers, most notably David Peterson. This meeting was his first experience with his counterparts, and he seemed relieved that it was over, that he had successfully made his points, and that he had withstood the pressure that had obviously been placed on him. He exchanged a quick word with Gary Filmon, Manitoba's premier, before we all headed back to the hotel. I was encouraged to note that Filmon seemed to be an ally — in contrast to Frank McKenna, who was waffling.

The conference opened at 9:30 the next morning. The premiers and their finance ministers sat around a large round table with the prime minister. According to the agenda, the open session during which the prime minister and premiers were to make brief opening statements was to conclude by noon, so that *in camera* meetings on various aspects of the economy could take place in the afternoon. In the end, however, the statements ran so far over their allotted time of fifteen minutes each that the session dragged on until mid- to late afternoon.

As I expected, the Constitution was the central issue. As the premier of Canada's newest province, Wells spoke last. (This is the protocol at every meeting of first ministers.) I was shocked as I listened to premier after premier defend the Accord and sling political arrows in Wells's direction. Only Gary Filmon and, to a small degree, Frank McKenna voiced any criticisms of the Accord before Wells spoke. Mulroney, for some reason, decided to respond to each premier's statement, mainly in an empty platitudinous way. He always took any opportunity to mellifluously thank the premier for his support for Meech.

By the time Wells spoke, I had lost all illusions that a constructive debate was possible. I hoped that he might depart from his prepared text to emphasize the constitutional issue more, given the obvious declarations of war by most of the other first ministers. If this was what his counterparts were prepared to do in public, I could appreciate what he must have gone through the night before at the private dinner.

I need not have worried. The premier read the entire constitutional section of the speech, while cutting back on other parts. But the most important moment that afternoon was his riveting exchange with the prime minister. Wells had argued eloquently that Meech Lake created a Canada with a class A province, a class B province and eight class C provinces. Incredibly, in his response to Wells, Mulroney made the same fatuous argument he had used on the telephone a few days earlier about the alleged exclusion of Quebec in 1982 as a way of justifying the Accord. Having listened to the premier firmly and clearly rebut that argument, I was astounded that Mulroney raised it again. Obviously, he had misunderstood and underestimated the premier; perhaps he believed that Wells would not try to contradict him in public. In any event, the moment Mulroney began to speak, I knew that the two were about to engage in a verbal duel that would have significant repercussions across the country and an electrifying effect on the growing popular support for Wells. As I expected, Wells forcefully argued that no province was entitled to special legislative status or to hold up the constitutional development of the country, whether in 1981 or 1989.

I have since met and spoken to countless people who saw the exchange either live on television or later in the newscasts, which replayed it often over the next few days. Without exception, they all cheered Wells on. Clearly, there was such a widespread and visceral dislike of Mulroney among the Canadian public that they were delighted that Wells was prepared to stand up to him and indeed firmly deflate him.

After this exchange with Mulroney, Wells called for the public to be involved in constitutional reform through a referendum. As Wells explained to reporters after the open session ended, when he argued that no one province should be able to hold up constitutional reform, he acknowledged that this also applied to Newfoundland vis-à-vis the Meech Lake Accord. But he pointed out that Meech explicitly gave Newfoundland a veto, and added that, nevertheless, he was prepared to put Meech to a referendum in Newfoundland should Newfoundland be the only province not to approve, in order to know the wishes of the *people* not just the government. If the people wanted the government to approve it, despite his own opposition, the government would follow the people's verdict. At the same time, he urged Mulroney to hold a national referendum. A rather startled Lowell Murray could only argue lamely that referenda were not the Canadian way.

The First Ministers' Conference was obviously where Wells established himself as the leading voice for Meech's opponents. It also provided him with a great deal of momentum. For me, the conference was where I discovered the depth of the opposition we were going to face from most of the major political machines across Canada. It was also my first direct experience with Canada's network of intergovernmental officials. Now that I had dealt with some of them, I knew we were going to have problems finding any allies at the bureaucratic level.

I had already met many of the bureaucrats socially the evening before. My first professional encounter with a specific subset of them was at a meeting of officials on Thursday evening in a suite in the Four Seasons Hotel. The purpose of the meeting was to discuss a possible communiqué for the first ministers to issue the next day on the Constitution. It was odd that the meeting was chaired by Patrick Monahan, representing Ontario, and that the federal officials arrived only just before it broke up. It confirmed that the feds knew that they had little credibility at this point and were relying on Ontario to take the lead — an incredible way to run a country.

At the meeting, I explained the province's position — that Newfoundland's rescission was just a matter of time. Even the most minor of suggestions in Newfoundland's alternative required an amendment to the Accord. Therefore, just as a mechanical matter, the amended Accord would have to be reapproved. Needless to say, the Quebec officials were less than happy. What was more disturbing was the almost complete lack of support from New Brunswick officials; certainly this was a sign of things to come. In general, my comments were met with either awkward silence or concern. Ultimately the meeting broke up without any conclusion being reached, and with each person taking a draft copy of a communiqué written by Ontario.

The premier had gone out to celebrate his fifty-second birthday with Mrs. Wells and their son, daughter-in-law and two grandchildren, who lived in Ottawa. Back at the hotel, I sat down and wrote a lengthy memo on the night's events. After consulting Robert Dornan, I decided to slip it under the door of the premier's hotel room to ensure that he read it before the next day's events.

On Friday, in an early morning CBC Newsworld interview with Don Newman, the premier suggested that he could agree to defer rescission provided he received a firm guarantee from all other first ministers that they would not proceed to approve the Accord as it stood, without permitting the current Newfoundland government to first review its position. Within an hour of the interview, Patrick Monahan came over to speak to me at the Newfoundland office on the main floor of the Conference Centre. With the transcript in his hand, he suggested that the premier's comments were inconsistent with my so-called "hardline" approach the night before. I pointed out that there was of course no inconsistency since at the officials' meeting we had only discussed the overall position of Newfoundland on eventual rescission. We had not discussed the type of interim agreement proposed by the premier, which only the premier and other political leaders could expressly address. In my view, rescission remained inevitable at some stage and there was little point in trying to defer the consequences by emphasizing that it might be delayed for a short period.

The premier's comment provided Mulroney with a face-saving way out of the meeting. After a long closed session on Friday afternoon, an apparently chastened prime minister finally emerged, to read out the following proviso to his announcement that Senator Murray would immediately commence a cross-country tour to discuss the Accord.

> The prime minister and all first ministers have given the premier of Newfoundland an understanding that the Meech Lake Accord or any variation of it will not be implemented until the legislature of Newfoundland has reconsidered the matter and expressed its approval or disapproval. In return, the premier of Newfoundland has agreed that the legislature will not, in the meantime, rescind the resolution already passed by the legislature of Newfoundland.

I immediately began to wonder what sort of manipulative use the pro-Meech forces might eventually make of this proviso. My fear was the nightmare scenario that Frank McKenna and Gary Filmon might fold under intense pressure from Ottawa and ratify the Accord in New Brunswick and Manitoba before the Newfoundland legislature could be convened to go through the rescission debate. Perhaps I was excessively suspicious, but I was definitely not alone in worrying about this possibility. Indeed, several members of the media persisted in asking about the mechanics involved in rescission and suggested that my nightmare scenario might become reality.

The November conference was where I noticed the first evidence of direct media manipulation. On Saturday morning, several major newspapers ran a story about how the premier had been prepared to announce immediate rescission in his opening statement but had been persuaded not to by, among others, Ontario's attorney general, Ian Scott. When I met with the premier, he was furious and in several media interviews that morning, he responded that nothing could have been further from the truth. When Ian Scott had come over to speak to the premier allegedly about rescission, the conversation had dealt only with provincial justice matters unrelated to Meech Lake. I personally saw every draft of the opening statement, and the premier had never once considered it necessary to mention rescission explicitly. One can only speculate about which officials planted the stories with otherwise reliable journalists — and about their motives.

Instead of immediately returning to St. John's when the conference concluded, I arranged to stay on in Ottawa to spend some time with family and friends. On Saturday, I had arranged lunch with Eugene Forsey, with whom I had been in regular contact since 1987. He was a delightful man — witty, compassionate, an amusing raconteur, and, of course, one of Canada's foremost constitutional scholars. In our correspondence and many phone calls, I was always amazed at the depth of his knowledge and the sharpness of his analyses. I learned a great deal from him.

I decided to ask the premier if he would like to meet Forsey and, in the end he, Mrs. Wells, Forsey and I all had lunch together in the Westin restaurant. Our conversation was lively and interesting, and Forsey obviously enjoyed it. The premier was characteristically modest when Forsey expressed his relief and admiration that someone had finally emerged to resist Mulroney's sell-out to Quebec nationalists. Forsey made a number of pertinent historical references that I'm sure the premier found as useful as I did. For example, he noted that in 1867 Georges Étienne Cartier always spoke about one *Canadian* nation (Forsey was thoroughly familiar with the Confederation debates) and that there was absolutely no historical foundation to the argument that there were two founding nations — the *"deux nations"* theory — or that Confederation was a compact among provinces simply to delegate a few powers to the federal government. At one point a passerby stopped to shake the premier's hand and congratulate him for confronting Mulroney, and Forsey commented enthusiastically that Wells was a true Canadian and entirely right in his opposition to Meech.

On Saturday afternoon, I finally had a chance to relax and went flying in a small Cessna with a friend. The flight above the Gatineau hills was spectacular, but of most interest was our pause, literally, over Meech Lake. (My companion practised stalling the plane at this point, which I thought was entirely appropriate.) I had spent most of the summers of my youth at a cottage on Meech Lake, and until the Accord appeared, I had always remembered them happily. One of my regrets is that Meech Lake became indelibly attached to the Accord and to all the negative associations that went with it.

On Sunday, I returned to the more relaxed atmosphere of St. John's. It felt as if we were in a brief lull before another storm, with none of us certain about where we were headed. A few days later, the first of many enormous waves of correspondence began to arrive from across Canada in response to Premier Wells's exchange with the prime minister at the conference. This one was so overwhelming that I really did not turn my mind to how to deal with it until shortly before Christmas.

One fax in particular provided some light relief. Shortly after our return, the premier received a copy of a cartoon from the Vancouver *Province* showing a back view of Wells urinating into Meech Lake, with Mulroney by his side. It arrived with a hand-written note that read, "Clyde, is that you?" and was signed by Bill Vander Zalm. We all had a good laugh. Certainly it confirmed the "Governor Moonbeam" image of British Columbia's premier.

Wells wanted each letter that he received to be answered in some direct way, except for the obviously bigoted anti-Quebec, anti-French ones. Ultimately we established a system whereby I would read and file the supportive letters each day according to province or territory. These letters would then receive a short reply from the premier signed by the automatic signature arm. I would also identify special letters from academics and from others who had specific requests; all of these would get detailed personalized replies from the premier. The pro-Meech letters, of which there were very few, always received special attention and a substantive letter setting out the province's position.

The anti-Quebec letters — the "radical" letters as I called them for easy reference — received a reply only from me. My reply did not say that it was written on behalf of the premier, since we had decided that everything possible should be done to distance him from any accusations that he was encouraging anti-bilingualism. My letter started out: "It appears that you have misunderstood the position of the government of Newfoundland and Labrador on the Meech Lake Accord ..." In order to ensure that no letters slipped through the cracks, all replies from the premier also emphasized "the government's belief that raising the level of bilingualism has a unifying impact and should be encouraged ..."

I was unprepared for the responses to my "radical" letter. I was accused of everything from being a communist to illegally opening the premier's "personal and confidential" mail. (To this day, it still amazes me how many people believe that the premier must read and reply personally to all correspondents!) A few frustrated people even went to the effort of obtaining the premier's home address and writing to him there, asking him whether my letter indeed reflected the government's views. They then received a response directly from the premier saying that yes indeed, my letter did accurately reflect the government's position. From time to time I found this entertaining.

At one point, I did try to eliminate the angry responses by softening the letter somewhat and enclosing a copy of one of the premier's speeches with a section highlighted that dealt with his commitment to bilingualism and to the Charter. Soon after, a woman called the office to congratulate the premier and then solemnly advised the receptionist to warn him that he had "an enemy working in his office" by the name of Deborah Coyne. When the premier was a guest on a Winnipeg hotline show in February 1990, I almost fell off my seat when a caller mentioned receiving one of my letters and asked whether I was authorized to write the response. Fortunately, the premier said yes without blinking an eye.

The "radical mail" was only a minuscule part of the 30,000 letters the premier received between November 1989 and July 1990. The vast majority of writers supported him fully and expressed their pleasure that the country finally had a principled politician who had the courage of his convictions. Typically, the letters implored the premier to "hang in."

As the months passed and I experienced various degrees of exhaustion, I sometimes asked myself whether I should continue to put so much time into answering the mail. But my doubts never lasted long. I was satisfied that the correspondence was not adversely affecting my other activities and convinced that it was essential for the premier to stay in touch with his popular support across the country. His replies demonstrated the premier's commitment to ensuring that the views of ordinary people were heard in the constitutional reform process. From my experience with the Canadian Coalition on the Constitution prior to my arrival in St. John's, I knew how much it comforted those frustrated Canadians to receive a direct response from someone who was in a position to articulate their concerns and their vision of Canada.

One outcome of the First Minister's Conference in November was that Lowell Murray made a tour of the provincial capitals and met with his counterparts on a bilateral basis. As the minister responsible for intergovernmental affairs, Wells was his counterpart in Newfoundland.

The meeting with Murray took place in St. John's in the government caucus room on December 8. Also attending were Norman Spector, the secretary to cabinet for federal-provincial relations, and Mary Dawson and David Paget from the FPRO. Not surprisingly, neither the premier nor anyone else in the Newfoundland contingent — most notably the justice minister, Paul Dicks — had any real sense of what Murray or Spector intended to accomplish. From my perspective, I hoped that a direct exchange with Wells might convince Murray of the depth of Newfoundland's opposition and persuade him to advise Mulroney to make a face-saving but responsible national statement to the effect that the Accord had to be reopened and that negotiations would have to continue.

We sat down in the caucus room, and Murray agreed that the premier should take us through Newfoundland's alternative accord. Murray is a stiff, expressionless man who can be excessively solemn and intense when he speaks. Spector is more animated but equally inscrutable. Journalist Andrew Cohen has described Spector accurately as "wily, masterful and occasionally abrasive. In the constitutional campaign he was the choreographer." While seated at the table with Murray and Spector, I had the uncomfortable feeling that the pair of them were playing cards with their hands carefully concealed, constantly on the look-out for ways to manipulate Wells into dropping his opposition to Meech.

Several things about the meeting disturbed me. One was that Murray focused on the premier's suggestion that an add-on to the Accord could deal with any concerns about the special legislative status. (This was the add-on that would state that nothing in the distinct society provision gave Quebec any powers that other provinces did not have.) I had fully expected this issue to come up, although of course I had hoped it would not. The subject was raised just before we ended the formal part of the meeting and broke for lunch. Fortunately, the premier wound up the discussion by reminding Murray that he would much prefer that the recognition of Quebec as a distinct society be placed in the preamble. Nevertheless, my guard was up.

A second disturbing development occurred at lunch. We briefly discussed the immigration provisions, which unfortunately always somehow got lost or relegated to bottom priority in any meeting. I pointed out to Spector that the provisions might permit all provinces to conclude and entrench in the Constitution agreements similar to the one being offered to Quebec, which wanted increased control over immigration. I also argued that it appeared to give the provinces at least the potential right to control the selection of immigrants *from within Canada.* This, along with the many flaws in the provisions, guaranteed the emasculation of the federal government's role in immigration. Spector acknowledged the specific provision, but then commented blithely to the effect that the feds just would not sign any agreement containing it with any province other than Quebec. I was shocked. This response — that the Constitution could be treated like a flexible corporate by-law — confirmed all my worst fears about the federal approach to constitutional reform. That the federal government would agree to give the provincial governments certain constitutional rights while at the same time publicly admitting that it did not intend to respect them is incredible. A more irresponsible position would be hard to find.

In any event, the meeting with Murray and Spector was inconclusive. Although both sides exchanged positions and, for example, debated the Newfoundland interpretation of the distinct society clause, I did not get the impression that Murray was really interested in exploring some of Newfoundland's alternative proposals with the other provinces. Murray did, however, suggest that the premier himself try out some of his ideas on other premiers. In the coming months, he proceeded to do precisely that; he accepted speaking engagements across the country over the ensuing two to three months, while also having bilateral meetings with various premiers.

The intensity of the national debate seemed to moderate with the approach of Christmas — a welcome development. The premier could now concentrate on the fisheries crisis, and I could attack the immense correspondence backlog.

But it was certainly not a "break." With the assistance of four employees of a small word-processing company and three high school students who agreed to fold and seal correspondence, I worked every day and almost every night except for Christmas Eve and Christmas Day. There were even seven of the "team," as we called ourselves, in the office until almost midnight on New Year's Eve. Despite the absence of any holiday, with the correspondence finally under control by early January, I was able to focus more clearly on the next set of challenges from the pro-Meech forces.

FOUR

The Pro-Meech Forces Regroup

PREMIER WELLS HAD THREE speaking engagements in mid-January; they proved to be a good follow-up to the First Ministers' Conference. The first, on Tuesday, January 16, was sponsored by the University of Toronto's Department of History and Students' Association. A few days earlier we had discussed whether the premier should give prepared speeches. He definitely prefers speaking without notes and is very good at it. But both Judy Foote and I agreed that, at least for some speaking engagements, a prepared text would be useful as a means to ensure that interested people could learn more about his views. We had already literally hundreds of requests for copies of his correspondence with the prime minister and for copies of Newfoundland's alternative proposals.

The premier decided that a prepared text would not be necessary for the U of T speech; instead, he planned to produce one for a Montreal engagement three days later. But on January 6 he received a bombastic letter from Robert Stanfield and Jack Pickersgill attacking his position. Stanfield was a former leader of the federal Tories; Pickersgill had been a Liberal cabinet minister. The premier decided that at U of T he would release publicly the text of his written reply to Stanfield and Pickersgill and then ad lib his speech based on the correspondence.

The premier's strategy to respond publicly to Stanfield and Pickersgill was a good one. They had already released their letter to the media and had been given some significant coverage. Many people saw the letter as a bitter personal attack on the premier and questioned the propriety of the authors' veiled threats against Atlantic Canada. For example, the concluding sentence in their letter apocalyptically stated, "It is almost beyond belief that any Atlantic premier would for no reason based on fact, expose Atlantic Canada to even greater difficulties than its people already face, much less give encouragement to those who would break up Canada." The premier was especially disturbed by their threatening tone, which he considered totally irresponsible, in that it contributed absolutely nothing to an informed moderate debate on the substance of the Accord.

The premier's reply to Stanfield and Pickersgill was completed late on January 15, which left Rosie Frey and me just enough time to make some fifty copies to take with us to distribute in Toronto the next day. I also worked late to ensure that the French translator received the final copy and to make arrangements to have the translation attached to the English version as soon as possible. The premier was very insistent that any major speech or public document like this be translated into French; he wanted to be sure that Quebeckers were aware of what he was saying.

Early the next morning, the premier, Robert Dornan and I boarded a direct flight to Toronto. The weather in St. John's was the usual rainy snow with a lot of wind, but the flight left almost on time. Then, however, my nightmare scenario unfolded — Pearson airport in Toronto was fogged in, and we were diverted to Dorval airport outside Montreal. At around 11 a.m., as we sat on the tarmac, Robert used a cellular phone to try to arrange alternative transport. Since the U of T speech was not scheduled until 4 p.m., there was a chance we could still make it by hiring a car, although none of us particularly looked forward to the long drive. Fortunately some sixty minutes later, word came that the fog had lifted sufficiently at Pearson that we could land there.

We arrived just in time to get a lift from a member of the Ontario Provincial Police directly to the University of Toronto's Department of History. (Apparently it is protocol in Ontario for the premier's office to arrange OPP assistance when another premier visits Ontario.) A casual luncheon had been arranged with some of Toronto's academics, such as historians Michael Bliss and Ramsay Cook.

Our next stop was a quick meeting between Wells and David Peterson at Queen's Park. Peterson was his usual glad-handed, jovial, "Hi there, Clyde" self. The two men met in private for about an hour. Robert and I stayed in another room with one of Peterson's executive assistants. We were joined briefly by Patrick Monahan, with whom I discussed the premier's reply to Pickersgill and Stanfield.

Monahan was interested to find that the premier had also released, as an appendix to his reply, a legal opinion prepared for the Newfoundland government by a Toronto lawyer named Neil Finkelstein. This opinion demonstrated that the distinct society clause did give Quebec a special legislative status. Monahan seemed concerned that, as a result of this release, there would now be pressure placed on Ontario to release the legal opinion prepared by Professor Peter Hogg to which Finkelstein had made critical reference. I expressed surprise that the Hogg opinion was not already publicly available. My instincts, much like the premier's, are to presume that such things should be made public unless there are very strong reasons to keep them private. To treat Hogg's opinion as something private seemed excessively secretive to me.

The premier didn't have much to say about his meeting with Peterson. I suspect that much of it was simply a restatement of opposing positions. We barely made it over to U of T's Convocation Hall in time for his speech. Several hundred people were in the audience, and the media were heavily represented. The premier got off to a slow start, but ultimately used his reply to Stanfield and Pickersgill to make a number of punchy points outlining his opposition to the Accord. His arguments generated plenty of spontaneous clapping and ultimately a standing ovation.

He was mobbed by the media afterwards, but we managed to plough our way out fairly quickly to the waiting OPP car, which whisked us back to the airport for the flight back to St. John's. Part of the reason for the media crush was that Jean Chrétien, a candidate at the time for the leadership of the federal Liberal Party, had just made a major speech on the Accord in Ottawa. Some journalists suggested to the premier that Chrétien's position sounded similar to his own. I was encouraged to hear this, since I was convinced that Wells would have an easier time of it if he had an ally at the national level. After getting back to St. John's at midnight, I caught a few reports on the late-night Newsworld telecast. They seemed to confirm that Chrétien indeed had clearly bashed the Accord and outlined a credible alternative to it.

On Thursday night, the premier, Robert, Judy and I flew to Montreal for the next day's speaking engagement. After the experience with weather delays on Tuesday, I was relieved that we were leaving the night before. Mrs. Wells joined us, since she and the premier were heading south for a short vacation early Saturday morning.

Once again, we revised the premier's speech right down to the wire. I had written the basic draft, but as usual the premier made many additions and revisions. Even so, the translation was ready by Thursday, which was time enough to make copies for the media and for distribution in Montreal. I was pleased with the speech because it clearly debunked all the pro-Meech historical revisionism about how Quebec was allegedly "excluded" in 1982, and set out the flaws in the Accord in a no-nonsense way.

Friday was a busy day. In the morning, the premier had an interview with the editorial board of Montreal's *Gazette*. What an eye-opener! I was amazed at the hostility the premier met there, particularly from the editor, Norman Webster, especially considering the harm the Accord might do to Quebec's anglophone minority, which was the *Gazette*'s main readership. The following day, Webster revealed how utterly insensitive he was to public sentiment by starting his editorial comment on the premier with "Save us from principled politicians!" His view was that Wells's inflexibility would wrongly destroy the Accord. Yet principled politicians are precisely what the Canadian people want and what they are most certainly entitled to.

After the meeting with Webster, we headed over to the Bonaventure Hotel ballroom for the Canadian Club luncheon. The turnout was big, and as in Toronto, the media were out in force. Wells was joined at the head table by Pierre Trudeau, Eugene Forsey, and three former Liberal cabinet ministers, Marc Lalonde, Donald Johnston and Charles Caccia.

I sat at one of the individual tables with Robert Dornan and a few others. The premier's speech was generally well received, and his demand that the Charter's notwithstanding

clause be repealed at the earliest opportunity received spontaneous and sustained applause. Although the people at my
table supported Meech, they were all impressed by Wells's
sincerity and convictions.

Next the premier met privately with Robert Bourassa in his
Montreal office. This meeting lasted some thirty minutes. The
premier indicated at a press conference immediately afterward
that he and Bourassa continued to disagree, but remained on
cordial terms. Quebec's intergovernmental affairs minister, Gil
Rémillard, and his deputy minister briefly joined Robert, Judy
and me in an adjacent office. Rémillard is extremely cool and
aloof. All I recall is his ironic greeting to me: "Welcome to the
distinct society."

Our last stop, at 5 p.m., was the moot courtroom of McGill
University Law School. The room was full to overflowing. I
was impressed with the premier's stamina — despite the
gruelling day, he obviously enjoyed speaking yet again, this
time without a prepared text. His remarks were followed by
some tough but stimulating questions from both students and
professors. The audience was more responsive than the one at
the Canadian Club, and the premier seemed to enjoy this.

I returned to St. John's on the weekend while the premier
and Mrs. Wells continued on to their vacation. I spent most of
my time answering letters and considering how to deal with
the latest pro-Meech initiative — specifically, the emergence of
a number of pseudo-private pro-Meech organizations.

The first of these groups had contacted me in mid-Decem-
ber. It called itself the Association in Favour of Meech Lake,
and its members were Quebec businesspeople. It was led by
Claude Castonguay, a close friend and confidante of Bourassa
and a former minister in the Quebec premier's cabinet in the
1970s. Castonguay is a heavy-set man with an abrasive manner
whom I do not consider a truly committed Canadian federalist. My impression of him is that his world revolves around
Quebec and especially the business community, which is not
surprising, given his provincial government experience. When
he speaks to someone with whom he may disagree or who
does not accept his version of Canadian history, he becomes
condescending and visibly exasperated. Certainly, he was a
less-than-ideal person to serve as an envoy for the Meech Lake
Accord outside Quebec.

Castonguay's executive assistant was a Montreal lawyer named Bill McNamara. We knew each other from our bar admission days in Toronto in 1982–83. Perhaps this is why he had been designated to call me to set up a meeting with the premier sometime in the new year. This meeting was scheduled for February 7. From the start and with the premier's full knowledge, I made clear to McNamara the government's position that the Accord had to be amended and that formal rescission was simply a matter of time. I also suggested that it would be helpful if Castonguay and his group put equal pressure on Bourassa and the prime minister to exhibit some flexibility themselves.

I assume that Castonguay's group and the similar ones that subsequently emerged to defend the dying Accord were banking on the precedent of the successful pro-free trade blitz led by the Business Council on National Issues (BCNI) and its head, Tom d'Aquino. In part, Castonguay's group supported the Accord because its members were obsessed with the deficit and certainly did not object that the Accord significantly weakened the federal government's ability to regulate and intervene in the economy. (Decentralization allows business to minimize regulation by playing off one province against another.)

Clearly the business groups, like most of Canada's politicians, never appreciated the public's depth of concern with the Accord and its widespread distrust of all political leaders except Premier Wells and, later, Gary Filmon. Equally, they never appreciated Wells's personal stamina or his determination to put principle ahead of politics. This incredible gap between the hopes and expectations of the Canadian people and the responses of their political and business leaders is in my view one of the lessons most worth learning from the painful Meech Lake debate.

Soon after Castonguay's group contacted us, I heard rumours that Tom d'Aquino was beginning to gear up the BCNI again, and that a staunch pro-Meecher named Gordon Robertson, a former Clerk of the Privy Council, was going to be its primary spokesman. The BCNI, many of whose members also belonged to Castonguay's group, eventually emerged under the name "Canadians for a Unifying Constitution." Later, a third group, made up mostly of academics, and led by a couple of McGill law professors, appeared under the name "Friends of Meech Lake."

In late December, shortly after the call from McNamara, the premier received an open letter from Ghislain Dufour, the head of the BCNI's Quebec equivalent, the Conseil du Patronat du Québec (CPQ), urging him to support the Accord. Many of the CPQ's members also belonged to the Association in Favour of Meech Lake, so this letter provided an excellent early opportunity to respond with a carefully drafted seven-page response. In that letter, the premier set out the principles underlying Newfoundland's position, and its alternative proposals, and urged the CPQ to participate constructively and substantively in the debate. This letter was delivered in the first few days of January. I immediately sent a copy to McNamara and Tom d'Aquino in the hope that they would reassess their role in the debate before the positions became more entrenched. Needless to say, it had little impact.

I did, however, receive another call from McNamara shortly before the premier's scheduled address to the Canadian Club of Montreal on January 19. He relayed none too subtly that Castonguay very much wanted to meet briefly with the premier before his speech in order to moderate the premier's remarks. That Castonguay would presume to think that a private conversation could alter the premier's convictions and principles was incredible. I explained that the premier was fully aware of Castonguay's position and that it would not be a valuable use of time to meet before the speech. (The meeting with him for February 7 was already settled and confirmed.) I added that the premier's position and his substantive concerns with the Accord were based on principle and were articulated from the perspective of Newfoundland and Labrador and would not be affected by what Castonguay had to say. The matter was then dropped. But after the Canadian Club speech, Castonguay quickly found a soapbox and used it to criticize the premier and reinforce the image of him as intransigent, anti-Quebec, and so forth.

The premier and I had discussed all of these pro-Meech initiatives. He regretted the attempts to avoid all substantive debate about the merits of the Accord, but was undisturbed — he was sufficiently confident of his own views and of the widespread support for them. I have to assume that throughout the remaining months, the pro-Meech forces always thought that the premier could be ground down and persuaded to abandon his position. They therefore willingly and irresponsibly participated in Mulroney's game of high brinkmanship in the hope that a crisis atmosphere would undermine the critical popular support for Wells, which was continuing to grow with almost every poll, at least outside Quebec.

What was particularly disturbing was the increasingly relentless tone of the pro-Meech rhetoric, and the apocalyptic predictions that Quebec would separate if the Accord failed. History will undoubtedly record that it was these "federalists" who did the most damage to the Canadian national fabric, who fed the nationalist fires in Quebec by encouraging people to think that the opposition was anti-Quebec. As the *Gazette* journalist William Johnson pointed out, at least during the debates of the late 1970s and early 1980s there was always a presumption that federalism worked in Quebec's interests so that it was worth taking Lévesque's *"beau risque"* to pursue satisfactory reforms. But here we had the federalist spokespeople in Quebec building the case *against* federalism in the event of the Accord's failure and seriously undermining the federalist cause in Quebec.

Castonguay, McNamara, and some six or seven Quebec business leaders and members of the Association in Favour of Meech Lake arrived for their meeting with the premier at mid-morning on February 7. I was not expecting much. The day before, I had spoken briefly to McNamara and he candidly admitted that Castonguay did not expect to change the premier's mind, but had to come "for communication reasons."

The premier was tied up with the ever-worsening fisheries crisis in the boardroom adjacent to his office. I joined the association's members in the premier's office while we waited for him. The atmosphere was cool and our conversation stilted. We all studiously avoided talking about the Constitution until the premier arrived.

In the ensuing exchange of views, Castonguay and two or three others politely put forward the now-standard pro-Meech arguments: that this was the Quebec round, and that Bourassa could not change Meech because of the strong and vocal Parti Québécois opposition. The premier calmly rebutted each argument in turn, to the obvious exasperation of Castonguay. At one point, for example, the premier stated that the possibility that the PQ could take power was not a reason to rush to pass

Meech but, on the contrary, a reason not to put the distinct society powers in the Constitution which would then be exploited to their full destructive potential by any PQ government.

What struck me the most was the extent to which the Quebec business leaders were insensitive to the concerns of Canadians outside Quebec, particularly those in the less advantaged outer regions such as Newfoundland. In one memorable exchange, one participant warned the premier against reopening the Accord since this would result in new demands being put on the table and it would then take years to get a new agreement. He suggested that Canadians just wanted to put constitutional concerns behind them and let their lives and jobs go on as usual. There was dead silence for a moment. Then the premier graciously replied that, unlike the more well-off Canadians in central Canada, the people of Newfoundland and Labrador did not want their lives to go on as usual. They wanted to improve their relatively poor living standards and were concerned that Meech would further diminish their opportunities to advance.

This was a theme that the premier would consistently drive home in response to frequent patronizing comments by Bourassa, federal officials, and others that Newfoundland was just a basket case subsidized by other governments. The people in Newfoundland and Labrador do not enjoy living on handouts, he would reply. With the appropriate investments in education, infrastructure, and so on, it could be ensured that everyone earned his or her way in a dignified manner, and sterile subsidies could be eliminated. Yet this was never going to happen unless the outer regions were given a greater voice in federal decisions — such as through an elected Senate — so that they could encourage more regionally sensitive development patterns.

The Quebec business group also badly misread the premier himself. About a month later, McNamara and a Montreal businessman named Philip O'Brien returned to St. John's after requesting further discussions with the premier. I sat in on the meeting. It turned out they believed that the premier's opposition could be "bought off" by a change in the mandate of the new Department of Industry, Science, and Technology so that it included broader regional development responsibilities for all provinces rather than just Quebec or Ontario. (The premier has always been highly critical of the new department and has often used it as an example of undesirable federal legislation that an effective Triple-E Senate could block.) I was flabbergasted by their naïvete. Needless to say, the premier said absolutely not. It would be difficult to find a better example of the politics of manipulation or of the narrow frame of reference within which the pro-Meech forces were operating.

About the same time as the meeting with Castonguay in February, Stanfield and Pickersgill replied to the premier's Toronto speech and more or less repeated the views set out in their first letter. This time however, the premier decided that his hands were full dealing with his fellow first ministers at the official level, and that there was no time to engage in time-consuming side debates with private citizens. An appropriate acknowledgement to this effect was sent. A similar approach was subsequently applied to some of the other coordinated correspondence received from the various pro-Meech groups. An exception was made for letters sent to all members of the House of Assembly when the obvious intent was to undermine the premier's support in his own government.

For example, when Gordon Robertson first wrote on behalf of the Canadians for a Unifying Constitution, the premier sent a long, carefully drafted response and circulated it among the caucus, whose members had all received the Canadians for a Unifying Constitution's letter. Similarly, when the Friends of Meech Lake sent all MHAs a legal opinion signed by more than thirty law professors contesting the government's interpretation of the distinct society clause and the spending power provisions, the premier's response again was carefully drafted and circulated.

But when Gordon Robertson, Tom d'Aquino, and Jake Warren sent a letter addressed to all first ministers (though it was obviously targeted at Wells and Filmon) with some suggestions for add-ons to the Accord, I did not even start to draft a possible substantive response for the premier, as I typically would have. Coming as it did at the height of the Special Committee hearings on the proposed companion resolution in April 1990, there was only time for a detailed memorandum critiquing the substance of the letter. The premier ultimately agreed that I would just acknowledge receipt of it on his behalf. It was impossible and almost absurd to contemplate "negotiating" with private interest groups and individuals.

However well-meaning, they were obviously trying to fill the void in Canada's national leadership left by the Mulroney government's complete loss of credibility. At the very least, the development was sad and revealing testimony of the decrepit state of federal-provincial relations.

FIVE

The Western Tour

O N JANUARY 22, WHILE PREMIER Wells was still on
vacation, a bombshell arrived from Victoria, British
Columbia. It was Bill Vander Zalm's proposal to save
the Accord. The element that attracted the most media attention was a proposal to recognize each of the provinces and
territories as distinct through an explicit reference in the Constitution. While this is not entirely accurate since there was also
supposed to be a reference to Canada's distinct national identity, Vander Zalm's proposal was ridiculed as creating ten or
twelve "distinct societies."

From my perspective, the most disturbing aspect of the
proposal was the plan to "unbundle" the Accord and stage in
its implementation over a period of five years. As early as
November 4, 1989, I had written a memo to the premier entitled "Perennial Unbundling Nightmares." Up to this point
the Accord's supporters had always stressed again and again
that the Accord was a seamless web and had to be passed as a
package unanimously by all governments. This requirement
for unanimity was what gave Newfoundland the explicit right
to kill the Accord. The premier was always asking his critics
why on earth, if they didn't like unanimity in this case, they
were extending the requirement to yet more areas of constitutional reform — to the Meech changes to the constitutional
amending procedures.

But many knowledgeable commentators of repute had
noted since the beginning that parts of the Accord could be

passed under the general amending formula that required the approval only of the federal government and seven of the provinces having 50 percent of the population. Some even argued (wrongly in my view) that if the Accord was taken apart, or "unbundled," certain elements could already be formal amendments to the Constitution since they had the approval of seven provincial governments having 50 percent of the population. (Most commentators agreed that new resolutions of approval would be necessary.)

This unbundling with no need for new resolutions is effectively what Vander Zalm was suggesting. His proposal was based on a very shaky legal opinion prepared by a University of Toronto law professor named Katherine Swinton. He was also suggesting that the distinct society amendments could be accomplished with the approval of only seven governments under the general amending formula. I did not share this view: under the existing constitutional amendment procedures, anything that affects the use of the French and English languages is subject to the unanimity rule. In this I had some unlikely though upon reflection perfectly logical allies — Jacques Parizeau and the nationalists in Quebec, and certain Quebec constitutional experts such as Senator Gérald Beaudoin. Of what possible value to Quebec were the already vague powers offered by the distinct society clause if they could subsequently be amended by a combination of provinces and the federal government without Quebec? Not surprisingly, Parizeau weighed in against Vander Zalm's proposal, which was clearly based on the assumption that the general "7 and 50" formula applied to the distinct society clause.

Despite my own negative assessment of the legal basis for unbundling, there is no doubt that Vander Zalm's initiative gave credibility to the awful spectre and gave the media something to pursue in what almost amounted to a campaign to find new angles that would save the Accord.

Although a few friends commented that unbundling was politically impossible, and that I shouldn't worry, I did worry, and concluded that the best defence was offence. So I tried to sound the alarm as widely as possible among those people in a position to counter Vander Zalm's proposal. Required of course were two premiers, in addition to Wells and Filmon, who would be prepared to say no to such a strategy and prevent the application of even the general amending formula.

This was based on the very reasonable assumption that Frank McKenna had now left the anti-Meech camp.

Two obvious candidates were Vander Zalm himself and one of the other western premiers. Popular discontent with the Accord was growing daily in the West, as was support for Premier Wells. Both would be boosted by a series of speeches that the premier was about to make in Vancouver, Edmonton, Regina, and Winnipeg between February 12 and 16.

At noon on Friday, February 9, the premier, Robert Dornan, Judy Foote, and I flew to Calgary. The morning was a scramble, since overnight the premier had made some major additions to his speech on the Accord. This speech would be the basis for his remarks in all four western provinces. Nevertheless, with Rosie Frey's calm organization, we managed to complete work on the speech and arrange for copies to take with us.

After stopping in Halifax and Toronto, we arrived in Calgary around 9 p.m. Saturday, February 10 was taken up with a meeting on Senate reform organized by the Canada West Foundation. Among those attending were Gordon Robertson, Senator Duff Roblin of Manitoba, former B.C. Liberal leader Gordon Gibson, and Professor Alan Cairns from the University of British Columbia. The discussion was fairly detailed and intense on virtually all aspects of a reformed Senate from its composition to its election to its powers. While some of the attendees supported the Accord, all were impressed with the premier's grasp of the topic and the sincerity of his convictions. They obviously found it quite unusual that a provincial premier would take a day out of his schedule to debate substantive reforms with academics and others.

The meeting broke up about 3 p.m., and the premier, Robert and I caught an afternoon flight to Edmonton. (Judy went on ahead to Vancouver, where the premier was to commence his formal speaking engagements.) The premier had agreed to speak at the annual convention of the Alberta Liberal Party at the request of its leader, Laurence Decore, with whom he was on friendly terms. Decore was staunchly anti-Meech and his constitutional position was very close to Wells's.

The convention was in the garish Fantasyland Hotel, which certainly gave it a peculiar atmosphere. The attendance was good — in part because of Wells's popularity but also because the national Liberal Party leadership race was underway and candidates such as Jean Chrétien and Paul Martin were there.

The premier's dinner speech bashing Meech, which he delivered off-the-cuff, was a tour de force that was wildly applauded. Anyone there who doubted Wells's ability to sustain the Meech opposition must have been reassured.

Decore's brother flew us back to Calgary in a small plane late that evening, giving us a view of Alberta's bleak winter landscape. Since we didn't have to leave for Vancouver until mid-afternoon on Sunday, I spent the morning walking around Calgary in the spring-like weather. The obvious affluence was quite a contrast to St. John's and reminded me of the very real disparities that existed between the different regions of the country.

We arrived in Vancouver late in the afternoon and joined Judy at the Pan-Pacific Hotel. This was the beginning of four gruelling days packed with interviews, meetings, and speeches. Throughout, the premier's stamina was impressive; it was obvious that he thrives on constitutional debate and genuinely enjoys exchanges with journalists and others.

Monday, February 12, started at 8 a.m. with a breakfast meeting organized by the Vancouver wing of the Canadian Bar Association. Again, the premier spoke without a prepared text and was very warmly received by most of the lawyers present. From there, we went on to a meeting with Vander Zalm at his downtown Vancouver office. This was Wells's chance to comment directly on the B.C. premier's proposal to save Meech. Since Vander Zalm wanted his officials and his attorney general, Bud Smith, to be present, I also attended the meeting. In person, I found Vander Zalm to be exactly as the media generally portrayed him — Mr. Personality, with a great grin but little substance. He appeared acutely aware of how popular Wells was in British Columbia because of his Meech stand. In fact, he seemed to care more about ensuring that Wells did not publicly criticize his proposal to save Meech and further depress his ratings with the B.C. electorate than about discussing Newfoundland's position or his own proposal.

During the thirty-minute meeting, Wells expressed his doubts about Vander Zalm's proposal to recognize every province's distinctiveness, noting among other things that such a proposal, if accepted, would accentuate Canada's differences rather than bring its people together. While the issue of unbundling was not directly addressed, he also mentioned his view that most elements of the Accord required unanimous provincial approval.

After the meeting, each premier was to give his own press conference in an adjacent room. Vander Zalm wanted to ensure that Wells would indicate that B.C.'s proposal was at least worth looking at. One of his aides told me this directly. Knowing that the premier did not think much of the proposal, I was interested to see what he would say. In the end, he politely said that he would certainly have his officials look at it. I choked at this, since I knew he already knew what I thought of it. He then added immediately that he would equally consider any other proposal that came down from any other official or non-official source. Needless to say, this had the effect of downgrading Vander Zalm's intervention, which was not what Vander Zalm's aides had in mind.

After a luncheon speech to the Vancouver Board of Trade and an hour on the popular open-line radio show with broadcaster Bill Good, we all headed out to the airport to catch the late-afternoon flight to Edmonton. Here, on Tuesday, February 13, the premier gave various interviews and a well-received speech to a packed Canadian Club luncheon meeting and had a private meeting with Premier Donald Getty. Because the meeting was one-on-one, I waited in an adjacent room with the Alberta officials. Getty struck me as a very stiff and solemn man; I also noticed that he was uncomfortable answering questions at the ensuing press conference.

We barely reached the airport in time to catch a flight to Calgary for one more Liberal Party event. I went straight on to Regina, where the premier was due the next day to make another speech and meet with Premier Grant Devine. When I spoke to the premier about the meeting with Getty, I got the impression that little was accomplished, since Getty was strongly pro-Meech. The premier could never understand how Getty could have agreed to extend the requirement for provincial unanimity to Senate reform and still believe that meaningful — that is, Triple-E — reform could take place.

The premier, Robert, and Judy flew to Regina early on February 14. I met them in the lobby of the Hotel Saskatchewan before we all headed out to a meeting with Devine. He and Wells met privately for a few minutes; then both came out to join the Saskatchewan officials and me. Devine was friendly, folksy, and bright, but seemed to view constitutional reform not as a matter of principle but as a matter of "let's make a deal." At one point he earnestly suggested a possible trade-off between Senate reform and the notwithstanding clause — something along the lines that if Quebec would abandon its use of the notwithstanding clause to uphold French-only signs, there would be some flexibility on the issue of a Triple-E Senate. The premier, I think, shared my astonishment: without question, such deal-making would rankle ordinary Canadians, and in any event this particular trade-off was a complete non-starter.

The luncheon speech at the Rotary Club went well. Then, after the premier participated in another radio talk show, it was off to the airport for an early evening flight to Winnipeg and one more packed day on the road. The morning meeting of February 15 with Premier Gary Filmon was again private, but I had a chance to meet my counterparts in the Manitoba bureaucracy. For the first time, I actually had the impression that I was speaking to allies. Of course, I might have expected this since Filmon was turning out to be fairly firm in his opposition to Meech. I was not to meet up with Filmon's advisors again until the first ministers' dinner the following June, although I tried to stay in contact with them to exchange information.

After the last Canadian Club luncheon speech to a packed hall in Winnipeg — another success for us — we all caught a mid-afternoon flight back to St. John's via Toronto. Just as I breathed a sigh of relief that we had made it through the entire swing with no major weather delays, the captain announced that the Toronto-St. John's portion was cancelled due to bad weather in Toronto. So we had yet another night on the road in an airport hotel before arriving back in St. John's in the early afternoon of the next day.

I thought that the week away had been very successful, at least in demonstrating the popularity of both the premier and his views. Everywhere he went, people would stop to congratulate him; in airports, we heard people say, "Isn't that Clyde Wells?" Even the pilot on one of our flights wished him good luck in his opposition to Meech Lake. What was also clear was how approachable the premier was, how much he enjoyed talking to ordinary people, and how easy people found him to talk to. He wasn't at all intimidating, which is certainly a good quality for a successful politician.

Back in St. John's, a huge pile of correspondence had built up in our absence. Apart from this, my main concerns over the next few weeks had to do with my continuing fears about the unbundling initiative and the unfortunate spate of English-only resolutions in several Ontario municipalities.

About this time, I became aware of the unusual influence of a talk show host in British Columbia. Rafe Mair had been a Social Credit cabinet minister under Premier Bill Bennett. From my earliest days in St. John's, I had always enjoyed reading his almost-weekly no-holds-barred critiques of both the Accord and Vander Zalm and his vigorous defences of Wells. The extent of his influence became obvious in late January when there was an extraordinary surge in the volume of mail from British Columbia. As I read through the letters, I noticed that several of them indicated that Mair had urged them to write to the premier. To this day, I am convinced that Mair's program was singlehandedly responsible for a good third of the mail from B.C.!

In any event, the program also proved a good lever on the unbundling issue, since Vander Zalm was obviously not immune to public pressure. I discussed directly with Mair the possibility that the Accord might be unbundled. He quickly saw the danger and was able to sound the alarm in a number of key editorials. This provoked many British Columbians to write some interesting letters to Vander Zalm demanding that he not unbundle the Accord but rather withdraw his support. Many of these letters were copied to Premier Wells. One outraged couple even sent in their ripped-up membership cards for the Social Credit Party.

Some time later, on April 22, Wells received out of the blue a copy of a letter to the prime minister from Vander Zalm. Among other things, it objected to any unbundling without the consent of all first ministers, and insisted that his own proposal never contemplated unilateral unbundling. This about-face was a relief, although a fourth premier was still required to definitely prevent unbundling.

In February, the English-only resolutions of some Ontario municipalities began to make national news. Although organizations like APEC (the Association for the Protection of English in Canada) were obviously marginal, and although their activities were immediately condemned by most responsible politicians, a great deal of damage was still done, particularly in Quebec. Yet again, the media played an unfortunate role in all of this: otherwise insignificant (albeit unacceptable) events such as a bigot in Ontario burning the Quebec flag were given disproportionate coverage. The Quebec media would show the clip over and over, conveying a powerful negative visual image to the viewer and blowing the incident up out of all proportion.

The premier firmly condemned the English-only resolutions in speeches and interviews. But he also used them as further evidence that the creation of a special legislative status for Quebec would inevitably be destructive. He pointed out that the intolerance shown by groups like APEC was clearly spurred by Quebec's Bill 178 banning English on outdoor signs, and that such intolerance, however marginal, would be intensified if some future Quebec government used its distinct society powers to proceed with legislation more controversial than Bill 178. The inevitable result would be two linguistic enclaves or solitudes and the destruction of Canada's collective commitment to bilingualism.

As February drew to a close, I had the impression of marking time. There was no movement whatsoever from Ottawa, prompting even *Globe and Mail* journalist Jeffrey Simpson to ask whether the federal government had gone "brain dead on Meech." At the same time, the Quebec Liberal Party was threatening dire consequences should Meech fail. At its General Council meeting over the weekend of February 24, a constitutional committee was established, its main purpose being "the preparation of the political content of the second round of negotiations to begin after the ratification of the Accord." (The committee was eventually chaired by Quebec lawyer Jean Allaire.) Such a move, revealing that Quebec was preparing still more demands even if Meech was passed, was guaranteed to alienate Canadians further. Meanwhile, support for the premier appeared to remain strong, boosted by his visit to western Canada, and I looked forward to further opportunities for him to carry on the public debate.

SIX

The Motion to Rescind
the Accord

IN LATE FEBRUARY, PREPARATIONS were under way for the reopening of the Newfoundland House of Assembly in early March. I always assumed that barring some extraordinary movement on the part of the federal government, the motion to rescind Newfoundland's approval of the Meech Lake Accord would be introduced early in the session, so I did not press the issue with the premier. He already knew that I favoured rescission as soon as possible.

In the three months since the meeting with Lowell Murray and Norman Spector on December 8, neither Ottawa nor Quebec City had shown any signs of flexibility. The official line from Quebec City was as hard as ever, bolstered by loud support from Quebec's business community, and official contact with Ottawa was non-existent. Meanwhile, our ever irresponsible prime minister continued his frontal attacks on Wells, at one point resorting to the rather insulting French expression that the premier should *"se mêler dans ses oignons"* — that is, just stay out of the debate.

On several occasions in February, the premier considered writing a letter to Mulroney to notify him that Newfoundland was going to rescind the Accord on the grounds that there was no sign of any significant movement by Ottawa to bring about meaningful changes to it. I tried out a couple of drafts, but the premier never proceeded with them; other matters required his urgent attention, most notably the fisheries crisis.

But as the Throne Speech for March 8 was drafted and finalized with a reference to the forthcoming rescission debate, the premier decided that he must notify Mulroney, if only out of courtesy. On Saturday, March 3, he telephoned Mulroney from his home, which marked their first direct conversation since the First Ministers' Conference. Now that the feds were alerted, I was prepared for some sort of attempt to manipulate the premier. Sure enough, shortly after the Throne Speech on Thursday, March 8, the redoubtable Lowell Murray went on the airwaves to accuse the premier of being in breach of his undertaking at the November First Ministers' Conference. Murray argued that since consultations were ongoing, the premier must postpone rescission. How anyone could say that "consultations" were taking place was extraordinary.

With the announcement that Wells intended to seek rescission, the media once again became consumed with the procedural game of when it would be, what form it should take, and so on, staying far away from issues of substance. The premier had not decided on a firm date for introducing the motion to rescind, but we in the office all assumed that it would be sometime in March. In addition, the premier decided that if a referendum on Meech was to take place in Newfoundland — he had committed himself to one at the First Ministers' Conference in the event that Newfoundland was the only province not to approve the Accord — rescission should occur as soon as possible, in order to leave enough time for the referendum before the June 23 deadline.

New Brunswick's forthcoming companion resolution was still being worked on, and I assumed that Meech's manipulators would probably want to time its introduction so that it pre-empted or diminished the public impact of Newfoundland's motion to rescind. The aim would be to try to undermine Wells's popularity by portraying his position as intransigent and inflexible when compared with McKenna's "constructive" initiative to save Meech.

So I would have preferred to introduce the motion to rescind before the New Brunswick resolution was tabled. The premier disagreed. He had settled on Monday, March 19 or Tuesday, March 20, as the introduction date. But when McKenna announced that the New Brunswick legislature would reopen on Wednesday, March 21, the premier decided to wait until the day after, March 22.

Then out of the blue, Lowell Murray requested a meeting with the premier. This was scheduled for Thursday afternoon or Friday morning, and the premier thought it only polite to wait until after that meeting before introducing the motion. The delay would have postponed the rescission motion until the following week. This was one of the very few times when the premier's gentlemanly approach to politics frustrated me. I could see no reason to delay the start of the debate and could only read manipulation into Murray's visit.

Fortunately, yet another event intervened. On Wednesday, March 21, the prime minister's office announced that Mulroney had arranged time on Thursday evening on CBC to make a significant announcement on the Constitution. Both Judy Foote and I were convinced that this was more manipulation, and that it would be far better to have the premier introduce the rescission motion before Mulroney's speech. The alternative was to let Mulroney criticize the rescission in advance on national television and place his own spin on it. We sent an urgent message to this effect to the premier, who was then in the House of Assembly, and fortunately he agreed.

By 5 p.m. we were all working flat out to finalize the motion to rescind and a second document that would be tabled at the same time. Among other things, this second document set out Newfoundland's alternative accord in columnar form next to the original Accord, article by article, to demonstrate clearly that Newfoundland's concerns could be met while still addressing Quebec's demands. The premier and I had, up to this point, been the main people involved in drafting both the motion to rescind and the accompanying documents. As usual, the premier had a very clear idea of what he wanted in the motion and essentially drafted it himself. He did, however, ask the deputy minister of justice to assist us, primarily to ensure that the form was technically correct. By late Wednesday evening the motion to rescind and the accompanying documents were at the printers, and I breathed a sigh of relief since further delays were now impossible. The motion to rescind would be introduced the next day — Thursday, March 22.

Lowell Murray was informed of the decision to introduce the motion when his office called late Wednesday to confirm the premier's meeting with him and Norman Spector, which also was scheduled for the next day. It was agreed that they would meet at the premier's house at about 5 p.m. The location was chosen apparently because Murray wanted to avoid any publicity. In my view, it was also because he was now only reluctantly making the trip. His original intention had no doubt been to meet the premier before the motion was introduced. By arguing that he was continuing to "consult," Murray could further delay it. With that possibility gone, he might have preferred to cancel the meeting, but since he had initiated the idea and the premier had publicly welcomed it, he could hardly back out.

Late Wednesday afternoon, the premier also spoke to Frank McKenna, who apparently tried to persuade him to delay the rescission. For me, this was more evidence of McKenna's obvious co-option as the *de facto* head of the save-Meech brigade. Of course, conclusive evidence of this had been the New Brunswick companion resolution introduced earlier that day, and the announcement that McKenna was now prepared to approve the Meech Lake Accord without changes, regardless of what happened to the companion resolution, as long as there appeared to be substantial support for the latter.

In substance, the New Brunswick companion resolution was pablum — a pale reflection of the New Brunswick Select Committee recommendations and of the proposals put forward by New Brunswick officials in their meeting with me on February 8. Predictably, it simply tried to buy off the most vocal opposition. For the territories, it proposed future amendments to facilitate the creation of new provinces and to allow the territorial governments to appoint senators and Supreme Court judges. For women, it proposed that the guarantee of gender equality in section 28 of the Charter be sheltered from the distinct society clause. This would have done even more damage to all other Charter rights. For aboriginal peoples, it proposed that there be annual constitutional conferences and enhanced participation at various First Ministers' Conferences. For New Brunswick's francophones, it promised the bilateral entrenchment of their collective rights — something which in my view would have led to two New Brunswicks as much as the Accord would inevitably have led to two Canadas. And for francophone minorities generally, it included a provision for the federal government and Parliament to promote as well as preserve Canada's linguistic duality.

At this point, the worst was certain, to twist an old proverb. New Brunswick's officials and other pro-Meechers must have seriously believed that Newfoundland could be isolated and, better still, that the premier could eventually be persuaded of the merits of their approach. And indeed I suppose it was a credible strategy if you believed that, by refusing to approve the companion resolution, the premier would then have faced additional pressure from aboriginal groups, from his erstwhile allies in the territories, and from women's organizations who stood to benefit marginally from it.

In the end, this never transpired. Aboriginal and women's groups maintained their tough stands with respect to such central issues as the parallel recognition of Canada's aboriginal peoples as a fundamental characteristic of Canada, and the protection of the entire Charter from the impact of the distinct society clause.

During that frenetic Wednesday, I discussed my fears with the premier as I so often did. He listened, but then effectively dismissed them. Either he just could not believe that sensible people could think such a strategy would work, or he was so confident of the correctness of his approach that, even if I was right, he thought the strategy would eventually fail.

Late that afternoon, New Brunswick's deputy minister of intergovernmental affairs, Don Dennison, called to solicit my reaction to the companion resolution. In my usual way, I was blunt in my critique and dismissal of the strategy, but I also stressed, as always, that I was expressing only my own views which might or might not differ from those of the premier. The conversation ended abruptly, and I am virtually certain that its main points were immediately relayed through the intergovernmental network to Ottawa and Toronto. At the very least, it must have put an end to any last attempt to draw Newfoundland "into the loop."

Murray and Spector arrived at the premier's house around 5 p.m. the next day. The four of us sat in the living room for an hour or so before having dinner with Mrs. Wells. The meeting was cordial but unproductive. The premier outlined Newfoundland's alternative accord and proposed amendments. I am sure Murray and Spector were already thoroughly familiar with the proposals, and neither revealed the slightest interest in their substance or any willingness to persuade any other first ministers, least of all Bourassa, to consider them. Certainly this was a less-than-encouraging position for Canada's top federal-provincial relations officials to take. Their indifference confirmed for me that the original purpose of the visit had been to delay rescission. Now that it was inevitable, they saw the meeting as wasted time.

For his part, Murray gave the premier an advance copy of the prime minister's prime-time speech, which was set for that evening. Neither the premier nor I were surprised to find that Mulroney was endorsing McKenna's companion resolution and establishing a Special Committee of the House of Commons to examine it. This endorsement confirmed just how much co-ordination and manipulation was going on between Ottawa and Fredericton. I later watched Mulroney on television protesting, "I love Canada." My impression, like that of so many others, was that he lacked both sincerity and credibility. If he really loved Canada, he would have set aside the brinkmanship strategy.

Mulroney's unctuousness was matched only by that of Peter Mansbridge shortly afterward on CBC's "The National." After linking up with both McKenna and Wells for comments on Mulroney's initiative, Mansbridge made the absurd suggestion that perhaps Meech could be passed subject to a sunset clause: all its provisions would go into effect but would expire in, say, five years unless renewed by all parties. Apparently Mansbridge thought he could negotiate a deal on television.

If the premier weren't such a gentleman, he would have dismissed the suggestion as ridiculous. Instead, he replied that one should consider any suggestion and then raised some of the problems that this one posed. For example, if Meech died at the end of five years, what would happen to legislation passed under the distinct society clause, and to appointments to the Supreme Court made in the interim period? I found Mansbridge's suggestion absurd and could not believe that the St. John's Evening *Telegram* carried a headline the next day to the effect that Wells was willing to consider a sunset clause. The entire debate seemed to be entering a silly season.

From my perspective, the one non-Meech topic addressed during the meeting with Murray and Spector was of more significance. Just before we broke for dinner, the premier mentioned in passing the intensifying refugee crisis in the province. Refugees, particularly from Bulgaria, had been flooding off Aeroflot flights into Gander on a daily basis since

1989, and accommodations for them were now so stretched to overflowing that the province's ability to manage the inflow would soon result in health hazards to the refugees.

I had been following the refugee crisis for some time. It was a concrete example of the perils of having ten different provincial immigration policies, which is what the Meech Lake provisions would have inevitably created. Apparently the federal government had agreed to Quebec's request that the entry of Bulgarian refugees into Montreal be stopped. Presumably this was pursuant to the bilateral Cullen-Couture agreement, and is what had caused the diversion to Gander. As I mentioned to the premier and others, imagine what would happen if all provinces not only had this power, but in addition it was entrenched virtually for all time in the Constitution. Immigration chaos would be too mild a description.

As I sat listening to the premier describe the crisis and its overwhelming impact on the provincial social services budget, I was shocked that it had reached such proportions with apparent federal acquiescence. And I was even more shocked by Murray's assertion that he had been unaware of the severity of the situation. It astounded me that the minister responsible for federal-provincial relations had not been fully briefed on developments in such a critical area of intergovernmental policy, even if it was the direct responsibility of another minister, in this instance Barbara McDougall. Norman Spector at least made the constructive comment that the solution was to put an immediate visa requirement on travellers from Bulgaria, at which point I thought yes, but why on earth had the feds not done it already?

The answer was not long in coming, and it was the first concrete example of being "meeched" in Ottawa. On March 28, a few days after the meeting with Murray, Newfoundland's Minister of Social Services, John Efford, advised the premier that when he met with McDougall on March 5, 1990, she had deliberately linked federal assistance in the refugee crisis to a change in Wells's position. Apparently she had taken Efford aside after the meeting and said, "If your position on Meech Lake were different, you would have an easier time in talking about the situation in immigration and perhaps fisheries and other matters."

The premier was shocked and angry, and immediately faxed a letter of protest to the prime minister. In it, he scrupulously set out the facts and gave the prime minister every opportunity to deny that McDougall's comments reflected government policy. Presumably, Mulroney's handlers were sensible enough to recognize how McDougall's initiative could backfire if it became public, and Mulroney phoned the premier the next day to say McDougall was not reflecting government policy. Some financial assistance was soon forthcoming, together with the appropriate change in the visa requirement to restrict entrants. But there can be little doubt that McDougall's actions simply made explicit what was going on implicitly, and I would have preferred the premier to have immediately gone public with it. Eventually, some weeks later, the story did leak out in a Toronto newspaper and received some coverage. Only then did the premier publicly and very mildly rebuke the federal government.

The debate on rescinding the Accord began on the day of introduction, March 22, and lasted until 1 a.m. April 6, when the government finally invoked closure to bring it to an end. The opposition's support for the Accord and its call for public hearings on rescission were predictable. I will always remember how eloquently many government members articulated their vision of Canada and their concerns with the Accord. No one could doubt now that Wells had the support of his caucus.

The only sour note involved an unfortunate comment by the finance minister, Hubert Kitchen, that Newfoundland had Quebec "by the short hairs" on Meech Lake, the implication being that Newfoundland was opposing the Accord merely to gain bargaining leverage over Quebec on the Churchill Falls contract. (In the late 1960s the Newfoundland government had agreed to a long-term contract to sell electricity to Quebec at prices that turned out to be vastly below market level.) The premier immediately denounced Kitchen's comment and called Robert Bourassa to apologize directly and to reassure him that the minister's comment in no way reflected government policy. It would have been only fair for Bourassa to acknowledge the gesture and put an end to the inevitable Newfoundland-bashing in the Quebec media. He didn't. The province's media would play up the statement and twist it to suggest that Newfoundland's opposition to the Accord had crass financial motives. It is clear that few other of the current political leaders operated according to the same principles as Premier Wells.

The only other unexpected development during the debate was that the opposition challenged the constitutionality of passing a simultaneous resolution at the same time as a resolution to rescind. The simultaneous resolution bound the government to respect the results of a provincial referendum on the Accord that would be held if Newfoundland ended up being the only province to oppose the Accord. Without elaborating on the legal arguments, I must admit that the constitutionality was at least debatable. (Constitutional jurisprudence indicates that a democratically elected legislature cannot absolutely bind itself to respect the results of a referendum.) I regret not having anticipated the position, because the solution was simple: separate the two resolutions. This separation would have forced the opposition to challenge only the referendum in court — an initiative that I am certain would have been quickly abandoned, since the political fall-out would have been heavy: Newfoundlanders and Labradorians were all in favour of having a direct say in their constitutional future.

With the two resolutions linked, however, the opposition plan was clearly to continue the rescission battle in the courts in order to gain some popular support, even if ultimately the legal arguments would fail. Presumably it was expected that this would complement other federal initiatives to undermine public support for the premier.

When I spoke to the premier about the opposition's strategy about a week into the debate, he was not particularly perturbed by the prospect of a court challenge, since his legal instincts told him that it would likely fail. This was also the conclusion of a Department of Justice legal opinion that I requested. But I continued to be concerned about the unpredictable political fall-out that might result from the challenge at this critical point in the debate.

In the evening of April 4, the day before the scheduled vote on the motion, the premier decided to call the opposition's bluff: without warning, he offered to sever the two resolutions. The House would vote on the motion to rescind; then it would vote on another motion dealing with the referendum, as well as establish a special committee to hold open hearings into the Meech Lake Accord, the Newfoundland alternative and other constitutional issues. As I predicted, the opposition's leader, Tom Rideout and its chief critic, Lynn Verge, were taken by surprise and immediately rushed out of the House, presumably to consult with their federal counterparts, with whom they were obviously working closely. Ultimately, the premier and Rideout agreed to defer the issue until after they met the next morning.

That night, I drafted the two separate motions, though I had no confidence whatsoever that the opposition leader would go along. Sure enough, by the next morning, the opposition had realized that the manoeuvre would effectively eliminate the political reasons for their court challenge — since they would only be attacking the referendum and not the entire rescission motion — and that in the circumstances a court challenge would only serve to boost the government's standing. So the opposition leader turned down the offer and the debate continued on the combined resolutions until expiry of the time set by the closure motion.

On April 5, shortly before the vote on the rescission motion in the early hours of April 6, the Quebec National Assembly unanimously passed a motion reiterating that the Meech Lake Accord must be passed as it stood. This was in response to the Quebec nationalists' hysteria about the New Brunswick companion resolution and the possibility that Meech might be reopened. That Meech was dying could not have been more obvious. Yet the manipulations continued.

While talking to Wells shortly afterwards, David Peterson hastened to point out that the Quebec Liberals had used some conditional language that could be interpreted as a willingness to eventually contemplate some indirect changes to elements of the Accord, but only if it was passed unanimously before June 23. This was just one of several attempts by the Quebec government and pro-Meechers to take a "nudge-nudge, wink-wink" approach to the constitutional crisis. Bourassa was cornered politically by the nationalists, but if we trusted him and passed Meech now, he would agree to changes later. The possibility of this seemed so remote that it was surprising that anyone was giving it serious consideration.

Given Bourassa's record and the strength of his commitment with respect to other tough promises — most notably his 1985 election promise to permit bilingual signs — it was reasonable to doubt his credibility. Moreover, at this point I increasingly felt that most Quebec officials really did not want the Accord any more and were at the very least not going to do anything positive to save it. They knew it was dying outside Quebec and, in any event, Quebec élites had always wanted much more than Meech offered. Why waste energy and political capital on the losing side of the battle? That this was Quebec's attitude seemed to be confirmed a week later when, on April 14, after an invitation by the *Globe and Mail*, Bourassa refused to submit an open editorial to run side by side with one by Wells because, according to Bourassa's press officer, Mr. Wells "is an extremist." (Bourassa's comment was quoted by the *Globe* editors as their explanation for having to use just an excerpt of one of Bourassa's earlier speeches, while Wells had sent in something special.)

Wells was surprised by the press officer's comment, since he continued to believe and to operate on the assumption that Bourassa spoke in good faith and was still trying to compromise. Indeed, at first the premier preferred to believe that the "extremist" comment could not possibly have come from Bourassa. Then Judy Foote pointed out that no "press officer" in his office would ever have made a similar comment about another premier without his personal knowledge. Much to our periodic frustration, the premier's instinctive fairness almost always prevailed in situations like this. He was always reluctant to suspect manipulation or bad faith and didn't now.

Another sign of the unravelling of the Accord came on April 6, the day after the Quebec resolution and a few hours after Newfoundland's rescission. At a joint news conference with Gil Rémillard, the federal cabinet minister Lucien Bouchard angrily suggested that Canada would have to choose between Quebec and Newfoundland. Without a doubt, this will be recorded in history as one of the most irresponsible statements ever uttered by a federal politician.

The unfortunate episode also served to demonstrate the power of CBC Newsworld. The Rémillard/Bouchard press conference was carried live. Literally within minutes, the telephone lines in the premier's office clogged up with outraged calls from across Canada criticizing Bouchard and supporting the premier. I had not heard the comments. When I returned to the office after noon hour, I found a pile of telephone slips on which were scribbled such cryptic messages as "We choose Newfoundland," "Bouchard should be fired," and so on. Only then did I investigate the matter and discover what had happened. For the remaining two-and-a-half months of the debate,

"CBC Meechworld" as it was dubbed by some observers, would be not only a critical source of information for the premier, but a strong influence on the waves of telephone calls, faxes, and letters that continued to swamp the office.

SEVEN

The Charest Committee

T HE SPECIAL COMMITTEE of the House of Commons announced by the prime minister on March 22 was headed by Quebec's Jean Charest, a former federal cabinet minister. (Charest had recently been forced to resign from his post after he had telephoned a judge.) The Charest Committee was composed of federal MPs from all three parties and was directed to tour the country and hold open hearings on New Brunswick's companion resolution, primarily in key urban areas. From the beginning, it was clear that every attempt was being made to rig the witnesses: the committee ensured that pro-Meech submissions were made and encouraged pro-Meech witnesses to appear. It was equally clear that the federal government and the pro-Meech forces were counting on "Meech fatigue" among the disparate anti-Meech forces. They hoped the hearings would be ignored so that the "moderate, sensible" voices in favour of passing Meech with a companion resolution would dominate the process.

Their calculation that there would be "Meech fatigue" was definitely accurate. Most well-meaning and committed opponents of the companion resolution were inclined to ignore the rigged hearings rather than dignify them with a submission or an appearance. Indeed, this was the premier's own reasoning when he initially decided not to appear. He also considered that his appearance would break the convention that provincial premiers do not appear before federal committees.

Just before the Charest hearings began on April 16, the premier and I discovered that residents of Newfoundland and Labrador were being given only forty-eight hours' notice to send in requests to appear at the St. John's hearings, which were set for early May. Everyone was outraged. The premier decided to issue a toughly worded press release condemning the committee and calling for an immediate extension of the deadline. It was now clear that the committee's strategy was to come to St. John's, listen to a series of primarily pro-Meech presentations, and then argue that this somehow indicated that the premier's support in his own backyard was less than solid. More and more people began to urge the premier to appear for the sake of countering any of the pro-Meech spin doctors. One of these people was Bill Rompkey, a Newfoundlander and a Liberal member of the committee. Rompkey was sincere and committed, as well as anti-Meech; throughout the hearings he was very helpful in passing on copies of briefs submitted to the committee.

Eventually, in the last week of April, the premier decided to accept the invitation to appear at the St. John's hearings on May 1, especially since other premiers such as Ghiz and Peterson were going to appear as well. Meanwhile, controversy and acrimony were embroiling the committee at every stop, in Yellowknife, Vancouver, Winnipeg, and so on. Numerous witnesses, having been offered what Global TV czar Izzy Asper succinctly called "leftover status" — that is, three-minute slots at the end of the day — engaged in shouting matches with the chairman. These incidents provided some colourful "sound bites" for CBC Newsworld — but what a travesty of the democratic process.

For me, the most egregious example of the committee's less-than-balanced operations occurred in Vancouver. Eugene Forsey was spending a few weeks there at the time the committee arrived, and during one of my telephone conversations with him, he told me that he had decided to submit a brief and make an appearance. Incredibly, when he took in his brief, he was told by the committee clerk that he had missed the deadline and would not be able to appear. When I relayed this to the premier, he decided that we should arrange for Forsey to visit St. John's so that he could present his brief there. The committee had the political sense not to make a bad situation worse, and agreed to Forsey's appearance. In the end, Forsey appeared on May 1, the same day as the premier.

The premier and I worked late into the evening of April 30 to complete the written submission that he would take to the hearings the next day. To my discomfort, the premier decided to set out explicitly the possibility that Newfoundland's concerns could be met by add-ons or amendments to the Accord. Two weeks earlier, he had asked me to consider drafting a set of add-ons that in theory could address the province's concerns. The occasion for his request was a forthcoming meeting with David Peterson. The premier was feeling more and more the pressure from Peterson and other first ministers, who implicitly or explicitly were portraying him as inflexible.

My immediate response to the premier, which I later backed up with a memo, was that I really could not do it. Drafting contorted add-ons did not make sense to me philosophically, intellectually, or in any other way. As a result, the premier himself did the first draft. When I had an opportunity to review it, I was relieved to see that the add-ons were significant and really highlighted the absurdity of the approach.

Now he contemplated tabling these add-ons with the committee. I strongly recommended against it and he agreed. I was relieved that his general reference to add-ons at least included a number of important caveats — for example, the statements that the companion resolution incorporating the add-ons must come into force at the same time as Meech, that the distinct society clause had to be amended to ensure the primacy of the Charter and to ensure that Quebec received no special powers, and that a new expanded preamble setting out all the fundamental characteristics of Canada must be included. Nevertheless, I was not entirely satisfied. I was concerned that once the premier opened the door to add-ons, he might be "nickeled and dimed to death," as the saying goes. As I expected, the next day CBC's Wendy Mesley immediately zoomed in on this particular reference, and the media began to work the issue *ad nauseam*.

The premier was scheduled to begin his presentation before the Charest Committee in the afternoon. It was holding its hearings in a nearby church hall. Judy Foote, Robert Dornan, Edsel Bonnell, Liberal MHA Walter Noel, the premier, and I headed over by car around 2 p.m. Walter Noel and I sat on either side of the premier at the witness table.

The premier spoke by way of introduction for about thirty minutes. He then answered questions from the committee members for almost four hours. The first question, from a Tory MP named Ross Reid, was the beginning of what would turn into a sparring match between the premier and many Conservative members. Reid suggested that Quebec had gained nothing from the 1982 patriation of the Constitution. The premier immediately pointed out that the Canadian *people,* including Canadians in Quebec, gained a great deal from 1982's Constitution Act and the entrenched Charter, and that Quebec's concerns were specifically addressed in a number of its key provisions. Section 59 expressly exempted Quebec from certain minority language education rights in the Canada clause of the Charter and allowed Quebec to insist that immigrants go to school in French. Section 40 permitted any province to opt out with reasonable compensation when an amendment was made transferring provincial legislative powers relating to education or other cultural matters from provincial legislatures to Parliament. Clearly, both sections were of particular interest to Quebec. And section 41(d) effectively gave Quebec a guarantee of three judges out of nine on the Supreme Court of Canada, while section 38(3) provided for up to three provinces to expressly dissent from amendments that derogated "from the legislative powers, the proprietary rights or privileges of the legislature or government of a province." Finally and perhaps most importantly, there was the entrenchment of French and English as Canada's two official languages, side by side with minority-language and education rights.

Then one of the Quebec Tory MPs suggested that the impact of the notwithstanding clause was far greater than that of the distinct society clause. The premier immediately replied that this was wrong — the notwithstanding clause only applied to certain sections in the Charter, whereas the distinct society clause, if enacted, would apply to the entire Constitution, including the entire Charter.

In his discursive preamble to a question, NDP MP Lorne Nystrom suggested that the premier should have held hearings before passing the motion to rescind. At first, the premier did not respond to this, since Nystrom raised a number of other points at the same time. At that point, I happened to look over to where Judy and Robert were sitting and saw them making urgent hand signals to me. As I attempted to figure out what they were trying to say, Judy started pulling her ear. At this point, I was perilously close to bursting out laughing; I thought that perhaps the premier's audio plug had fallen out. Fortunately, I felt a tap on my shoulder, and a gentleman slipped me a note from Robert. They wanted to ensure that Wells replied to Nystrom's innuendo about the need for hearings. I quickly scribbled a note to the premier, and very smoothly, he went on to argue that since his predecessor, Brian Peckford, had never held hearings and indeed had avoided any real debate on Meech, rescinding the approval without hearings simply brought Newfoundland back to the starting point again.

Finally, Liberal MP Ethel Blondin asked with concern what the committee should recommend. The premier replied that the committee should conclude that much more public debate was required on the proposed reforms. And rather than make quick-fix substantive proposals, which would merely increase the present confusion and public alienation, the committee should propose the establishing of a national convention that would provide a democratic public forum for the reopening of comprehensive talks on the Constitution.

Not surprisingly, the sound bite that was most frequently broadcast was a non-substantive one: Bill Rompkey quite properly accused Jean Charest of "badgering" the premier during an exchange on immigration powers. To be honest, I never noticed it; I was used to Charest's pompous style by then, and the episode came toward the end of the four-hour marathon and didn't stand out at the time. But Rompkey's intervention was effective, and judging from the number of letters and faxes we later received praising Rompkey and criticizing Charest, the word "badgering" temporarily became one of the more popular words in our day-to-day lexicon.

I thought the premier had done brilliantly. He met every argument made by the committee members and was able to dispel many of the myths propagated by supporters of the Accord. In addition, he received several hours of intensive news coverage and was able to demonstrate not only his understanding of constitutional issues, but also the sincerity and depth of his convictions.

The hearings in St. John's wound up the next day with a series of five-minute presentations from individual citizens. Of these, an extraordinary 50 percent were in favour of Meech. As

Blondin colourfully put it, no one knew where they had come from — perhaps caves. But of course they were the core group of staunch pro-Meechers, who were launched again and again in basically the same formation, though always under a different name to give the illusion of strength — the Friends of Meech Lake, Newfoundlanders and Labradorians for Confederation, and so on.

I did not pay too much attention to the remaining days of the Charest Committee hearings. But one witness did attract my attention. On May 3 in Ottawa, a man called Roger Tassé surfaced. A slight, soft-spoken man, he had been the federal deputy minister of justice in the 1980-82 period, when the Constitution was patriated. In a less-than-subtle attempt to assuage Charter activists, the Charest Committee described him as a principal architect of the Charter. I assumed that Tassé, who had been seconded from his private-sector job to advise the federal government during the original Meech negotiations in 1987 and who was well-connected with pro-Meech constitutional élites and with some key advisors to Bourassa, had been deliberately recruited again to try to save Meech and to work the back channels between Ottawa and Quebec City. I was equally disturbed to learn that he had recently been associated with both Chrétien and his close aide Eddie Goldenberg in the same Ottawa law firm — a link which I also assumed would be used by the pro-Meechers.

Tassé was a spokesman for what has been referred to as the *"calmez-vous"* school of interpreting the distinct society clause; he made several recommendations whose point was "to reassure people by clarifying the Accord, without touching the Accord itself." His recommendation dealing with the spending power restrictions was meaningless: it merely stated that those restrictions would "in no way affect the government commitments outlined in section 36 of the Constitution Act." He was referring, of course, to the commitments to equality of opportunity for all Canadians. This guarantee was empty, since nothing was done to offset the massive disincentive to initiating new national programs that was implicit in the Accord.

Tassé's second recommendation was that a new provision stipulate that the distinct society clause was merely an interpretative clause that would work with the Charter and not override it. This provision would only be used when the courts had to decide whether a limit imposed by a government on our rights or freedoms was reasonable and "demonstrably justified in a free and democratic society." This tactic would prove to be one of the most deceptive yet displayed by the pro-Meech supporters and was to play a major role in the negotiations down to the bitter end.

It is vital to describe how the deception worked. On the surface the proposal looked great: it stated that, in effect, nothing in the distinct society clause could override the Charter of Rights and Freedoms. (The words "infringes or denies" would be used in the final version, which emerged in the form of a legal opinion annexed to the June 1990 companion agreement.) To the general public and media, this proposal would be seen as a major concession; indeed, the *Globe and Mail* and other media referred to it in laudatory terms as soon as it surfaced — to no one's surprise — as a key recommendation of the Charest Report on May 17.

Unfortunately, the proviso in the proposal is the key element and it expressly authorized what was at least only implicit or vague in the distinct society clause: that the Quebec government would be justified in passing measures perhaps similar to Bill 178, whether or not they infringed on our basic rights. In other words, the Tassé recommendation, if accepted, would have made it virtually certain that a future court considering Bill 178-type legislation would uphold it under section 1 of the Charter, with no need for the Quebec government even to resort to the notwithstanding clause. The Tassé recommendation or any variation of it would have done nothing to eliminate, and indeed would have reinforced, Quebec's powers to limit our rights and freedoms in a way that other governments could not. Effectively, it would have created different classes of Canadians and a hierarchy of rights.

Besides being deliberately deceptive, the entire exercise was a futile attempt to square the circle; it also avoided addressing the fundamental issues in any direct way. It was clear that Quebec wanted to be able to override the Charter's provisions on language rights and mobility rights, which are protected even from the notwithstanding clause.

For example, the Quebec government has indicated that it wants control over language matters and disagrees with any constitutional guarantee of access to English schools. In my view, this issue should be debated openly rather than dealt with in an underhanded way that debases the Charter, which belongs to all Canadians.

I was vaguely aware of Tassé's proposal shortly after he presented it on May 3, having read William Johnson's critical commentary on it in Montreal's *Gazette*. But I did not focus on the details until we received a copy of the brief out of the blue on Friday evening, May 11. That we received it directly from the FPRO was a clear signal the Tassé proposal was being taken seriously. (Later, Lowell Murray's office couriered the original to us — another first.) At that point I sounded the alert and immediately wrote a critique of the brief for the premier.

It was unfortunate that I did not get my critique to the premier before the weekend. Early Monday morning, I learned that over the weekend Jean Chrétien had presented Wells with what amounted to an add-on to the Accord in legal language that would accomplish exactly what Tassé was proposing. I was horrified. The premier quickly saw the connection and the flaw. This was to be the beginning of a whole new struggle in the arena of so-called add-ons to the Accord.

It was at this point that I perceived a link between Chrétien and the save-Meech forces and that a number of puzzle pieces fell into place. In early March, I had heard that a Montreal lawyer named Eric Maldoff, a former head of Alliance Québec, had prepared a document recommending that Chrétien support add-ons to the Accord by way of an "interpretative, procedural and supplementary protocol" annexed to it. In this scenario, Meech would pass unamended only on the "substantial assurance" that the protocol would later be ratified — whatever that meant. This interpretative protocol would state only that nothing "is intended to diminish the rights of Canadians under the Constitution," something that would do nothing to eliminate the widespread concerns for the Charter. Moreover, a further clause would be added to the Constitution to ensure that "the Constitution shall be interpreted in a manner consistent with: (i) the commitment of Canadians to fundamental rights and freedoms and the equality of persons as described in Section 15 of the Charter (ii) the rights of aboriginal people and the multicultural heritage of Canada and (iii) the equality of provinces." The latter proposal was just a Band-Aid on a Band-Aid and no substitute for the comprehensive Canada clause that had been put forward by Manitoba as a means to overcome the concerns about the distinct society clause.

When I received this material, I was concerned. But I hoped that the discussion was still limited to a few advisors and that Chrétien would reject the advice. Although I had always had my doubts about Chrétien's ability to maintain a coherent constitutional position, I was relieved after hearing his strong January 16 speech.

I was jolted out of complacency when Manitoba's Liberal leader, Sharon Carstairs, communicated by letter with the premier on April 4, the day before the scheduled rescission vote, enclosing the Maldoff document and suggesting that it might provide a way around the impasse. Only then did I discuss with the premier the likely source — Chrétien's advisors — and ask him whether he thought Chrétien had now concluded that Meech must pass and was getting directly involved. The premier replied that he did not know and indicated that he would likely speak to Chrétien directly.

I know that a phone call took place on April 5. The premier never really discussed the conversation, but I had the clear impression he believed that Chrétien was now waffling.

A few days later, the premier conveyed to Sharon Carstairs that he did not consider the document to be particularly helpful, mainly because it was just another version of pass-Meech-now-fix-it-later that showed little regard for those basic principles or fundamental precepts which are so essential to durable, legitimate constitutional change. This response assuaged my rising anxiety, but only briefly.

On May 17, 1990, we received a copy of the Charest Report. A quick glance at it confirmed my worst fears: it did not convey objectively and constructively the concerns the committee had heard. If it had, it would have recommended what the premier had suggested to Ethel Blondin — that the Accord be reopened, and that a new process be established to ensure meaningful public input, however long it took. The perennial optimist, I always had hoped that the committee would come to some sort of similar conclusion and put an end to the miserable process in which all of us were now entangled. At the very least, I had hoped that the Liberal and NDP members would issue a strong dissent and provide some support for Wells and Filmon. But this was not to be.

Instead, in a desperate attempt to achieve unanimity, the report's authors reduced all their recommendations to the lowest common denominator and avoided all stipulations as to the precise content or even timing of any amendments. For those familiar with the debate, there could be no doubt that the report was carefully crafted so that the feds could draft add-ons similar to those put forward by Frank McKenna, and so that Chrétien could embrace its provisions and continue his now-ongoing efforts to persuade Carstairs and Wells to support the Accord with a companion resolution.

It was now depressingly clear to me that Chrétien had decided it would be better for Meech to pass so that he did not have to face a constitutional crisis upon his election as leader in June. One of his envoys to Wells — self-appointed or otherwise — was Brian Tobin, a Newfoundland Liberal MP. Tobin is a witty man with a high regard for himself who appears to treat politics as a game. His efforts at manipulation were all too obvious. For example, the premier was kept informed of how the report was evolving in its various drafts, and occasionally spoke to Tobin and Rompkey — they initiated the calls — although to my knowledge he would always repeat his fundamental objections to the Accord. Nevertheless, Tobin began to convey the distinct impression to the Liberal caucus in Ottawa — and later *sotte voce* to the Newfoundland caucus — that he had a close relationship with "Clyde" and that the premier was favourable to the report and to "saving" the Accord with add-ons.

I can only speculate about who else besides Tobin was directly involved in the operation to use Chrétien's Liberals to influence the premier. It is up to others to contradict or correct me. But my understanding was that the federal government's contact with Chrétien's key advisors — John Rae, Eddie Goldenberg and Eric Maldoff — came via Stanley Hartt, the prime minister's chief of staff. Tassé was another direct link, having been Chrétien's deputy during the patriation debates and more recently a partner of Chrétien and Goldenberg in an Ottawa law firm. As already noted, Tassé was becoming a go-between with Quebec officials and the front person for the proposed add-ons to deal with the distinct society clause and spending power concerns.

On the same day that the Charest Report was released, the premier received another phone call from Chrétien, who again put forward the Tassé provision for dealing with the Charter. This time he persuaded the premier to consider it seriously as part of Newfoundland's add-ons. I considered Chrétien's involvement foolish — I was convinced that he could never change the premier's mind and that all he would do was alienate people on both sides of the debate.

Shortly after the Charest Report was released on May 17 came the announcement that Lowell Murray and Norman Spector would do a quick sweep of the provincial capitals. They met with Wells in his office in St. John's on May 21 — the day of Lucien Bouchard's sudden resignation. I attended the meeting, together with Barbara Knight. The purpose of the meeting was to allow Murray to seek sufficient common ground, among the "dissident" provinces in particular, to justify a first ministers' meeting.

Murray and Spector brought with them proposed federal add-ons to the Accord that were consistent with the Charest Report. I was not surprised that the language regarding the distinct society clause and Charter was precisely the same as Chrétien's in his contacts with the premier. This was all the concrete evidence that I needed that there was close co-operation between Chrétien's advisors and the federal government.

It was a subdued meeting. Murray and Spector reviewed their add-ons and the premier went through those of Newfoundland. (This was the list, prepared in April, that had not yet been amended to reflect Chrétien's suggestion a few days earlier.) Little else was accomplished, and it was clear that there was still a wide gap between the federal proposals and those of Newfoundland, not only in substance but also on the timing of the amendments. Newfoundland and Manitoba were both insisting that amendments had to take place at the same time that the Accord was implemented, while the federal government document stipulated that no amendment could be proclaimed until after Meech came into force.

My sense of unease rapidly intensified when I heard Spector blithely comment that the provisions relating to Supreme Court appointments and immigration jurisdiction were "off the table" — that is, non-negotiable — even though Newfoundland was proposing add-ons to deal with them. Clearly, this remark was just a form of direct pressure; even so, Newfoundland's isolation was obviously increasing. I knew that the federal strategy was to continually portray the premier's position as unreasonable, inflexible, and extreme in the face of all the "significant" concessions to Meech opponents. By portraying him in this way, the feds were hoping to undermine his support among the "Meech-fatigued" public, especially in Newfoundland and Labrador. If this happened, and if Manitoba folded on all key points, then clearly, even with the firmest resolve in the world, Wells could not likely hold out, and might even lose a provincial referendum.

Any chance, however, that the federal add-ons arising from the Charest Report might form the basis for a new compromise was soon lost as a result of events in Quebec. Hours after the report was released, both the Quebec media and that province's officials portrayed it as an insult to Quebec — as twenty-two demands by the rest of Canada (there were that many recommendations) that were the condition for agreeing to the original five moderate demands of Quebec. Even responsible journalists like *La Presse*'s Lysiane Gagnon were caught in the hysteria and never got around to examining the substance. All of this, and Bouchard's abrupt resignation on May 21, which was an unexpected and personal blow to the prime minister, reduced the feds' constitutional efforts to a state of total disarray.

After the meeting with Murray and Spector, the premier tried hard to move negotiations forward. He and Gary Filmon tried unsuccessfully to schedule a meeting with Frank McKenna. Their efforts would be pre-empted by the prime minister's sudden announcement that he would meet each premier individually over the May 25–28 period. In any case, McKenna's reluctance to attend had been all too obvious, which confirmed that he had joined the pro-Meech brigade. In the meantime, Filmon seemed to be stiffening his stand, especially on the need for Senate reform. I was encouraged but somewhat suspicious: if he insisted on immediate Senate reform as some optimistic Manitobans suggested to me, Meech was dead. But I could not believe he could suddenly be so hardline; I was certain that if his new attitude was genuine, it was just a temporary bargaining position to deal with internal pressures.

On May 24 the premier decided to table the Newfoundland add-ons in the House of Assembly, thus making them public. This was consistent with his strong view that negotiations could not go on in secret. He also sent copies to all the premiers, to Manitoba's opposition leaders, Sharon Carstairs and Gary Doer, and to the two territorial leaders.

Much to my chagrin, the premier next decided to write to Murray, at the same time substituting Tassé's Charter provision — with a slight modification that strengthened the Charter protection moderately, though in no way sufficiently — for Newfoundland's original add-on. The original had been much more effective in protecting the Charter. The premier did, however, stress that this add-on must be tied to the "powers and jurisdiction" add-on, which would greatly limit Quebec's ability to justify legislation that infringed on Charter rights (under section 1 of the Charter), since such legislation would only be possible if every other government had the same power or jurisdiction, which most of the time would not be the case. My sense of unease was escalating. I could not understand why the premier was compromising even to this degree when it seemed obvious that the federal government was not the least bit interested in really accommodating his concerns.

Mulroney held his private meeting with the premier at 24 Sussex Drive in Ottawa on Sunday, May 27. Ostensibly, it was held so that Mulroney could decide whether there was "sufficient progress" to justify some sort of first ministers' meeting. Yet again, I naïvely believed that the time had finally come when the prime minister would take the responsible step of announcing the reopening of the negotiations and the elimination of any deadline. It certainly did not appear that Mulroney had any idea about what else to do next, or any back-up plan in the event that Meech failed. As always, he lacked any coherent, principled vision of the country.

After that meeting, Norman Spector handed Wells a new federal working document, which he passed on to me the next day in St. John's. The premier and I both agreed that it was a definite regression to a pre-Charest Report state of affairs, especially with respect to the distinct society/Charter issue. It referred only to possible clarifications to the Accord; the reference to a specific amendment to the distinct society clause that had been part of a similar document only a week earlier was no longer there. In addition, the controversial term "override," which would have ensured that the distinct society clause did not "override" the Charter, had been deleted — a clear indication that the feds had capitulated to Bourassa's fear of a nationalist backlash in Quebec if he made any concession on the issue of the Charter.

The feds were now back to their old strategy of placing intolerable pressure on Newfoundland and Manitoba to pass Meech without changes, or at most with some companion resolution that might take effect sometime after June 23. And the old desperate accusations were surfacing yet again: that it was unacceptable for premiers to repudiate the signatures of their predecessors, that Wells and Filmon were purporting to reflect the concerns of millions of Canadians when they represented only a tiny percentage of the overall population. All in all, it was a depressing situation.

Much to my surprise, after a telephone call with Ottawa later on Monday, May 28, the premier informed me that a meeting had been arranged for the next day in St. John's with Lowell Murray and Roger Tassé. That Tassé would attend set off alarm bells, but I was really at a loss about what to expect. I could only assume that the meeting's purpose was to press the premier for more and more concessions. I was extremely worried: I believed that the premier was being misled by Murray into believing that Tassé was going to be able to get the Quebec government to make significant concessions.

The meeting probably represented my toughest moment in the entire debate on Meech. To that point, I had never seriously considered how I would react if the premier decided that he would have to accept the Accord. As I listened and rather numbly participated in the three-hour session, I was sure I was listening to a person who was ready to compromise sufficiently to save the Accord, provided the other first ministers, especially Bourassa, were willing to agree to certain add-ons.

Only four people attended the meeting: Murray, Tassé, the premier, and I. All the tough issues — the Charter, special legislative status, the unanimity requirements, the spending power restrictions — were addressed, and in virtually all areas except perhaps the issue of the veto over Senate reform, a consensus of sorts began to emerge between the premier and Tassé. I forced myself to recognize what was going on. Clearly, the premier himself would have to bear the heavy political responsibility if he killed the Accord, and it was entirely possible and human that he had decided he should not hold out any longer. My major worry at this point was that if the premier did want to negotiate amendments, parallel accords, or whatever, I was not in a position to give him the expert advice he needed. For the first time since joining his office, I concluded that intellectually I could not be a very constructive participant. I did not consider resignation, but knew I would have to share my responsibilities.

Early the next morning, I had a subdued discussion with the premier. I could not hide my concern and disappointment, but I made it clear that if negotiations had reached the bargaining stage, I would make sure he got the best advice possible, if, as I expected, I could not provide it. The premier listened quietly and agreed. A day later, on Thursday, May 31, Mulroney announced that a first ministers' dinner would convene on Sunday, June 3, in Ottawa. In accordance with our conversation, the premier agreed that I should arrange for Neil Finkelstein to attend. Finkelstein was the Toronto lawyer and constitutional expert who had written the legal opinion in December supporting the Newfoundland government's interpretation of the distinct society clause.

I have the greatest respect for Finkelstein and knew that Wells would find him invaluable. I never had any doubt that he would be loyal to the premier throughout the first ministers' meeting. But I was concerned that he was a reasonably close friend of both Eric Maldoff and Eddie Goldenberg and that he had helped to draft Chrétien's January 16 speech. (He was also on fairly friendly terms with Patrick Monahan, a key policy advisor to Peterson, and with his former employer, Ontario's attorney general, Ian Scott.) I worried that he might be innocently used by Chrétien's advisors and others as a means to exert even more pressure on the premier. As will be seen from what happened that week in Ottawa, my worries had some basis.

I was aware that the advisors to Chrétien and Peterson in particular saw me as a block to the premier, as someone who had to be "got around" in order to "get to" him. This is part of the reason why Chrétien used to call the premier directly, instead of getting Maldoff or Goldenberg to call me, which would have been more logical. (I know both men, and had spoken to Maldoff as recently as early January, just before the premier's speech in Montreal, when he expressed an interest in learning "what made the premier tick.")

I can only assume that these people somehow thought I would suppress information or proposals. Nothing could be more absurd. They obviously had no idea of how deep the premier's convictions ran and didn't understand the nature of my role as constitutional advisor. I would, of course, write comments and brief the premier on proposals and new developments, and undoubtedly this direct access to the premier might have given my views a preliminary advantage. But, at the same time, I never considered myself anything more than a direct conduit to the premier, and I never spoke on his behalf without his express knowledge and agreement. Most important, as was obvious to anyone who knew the premier even slightly, the premier had his own clear frames of reference when it came to analyzing proposals and ideas. If he "accepted" my advice, it was only because it happened to coincide with his own opinions.

In any event, as I expected, the Chrétien people saw Finkelstein as a new conduit to the premier. On Friday, June 1, Finkelstein called me to say that he had been contacted by Maldoff about his having joined the Newfoundland delegation. He wanted to know whether he could talk to Maldoff and Goldenberg directly. At least the fact that Finkelstein called me confirmed his loyalty. I immediately called the premier at his home — it was noon and he was having lunch — and spoke to him about the situation. I asked him up front whether, in light of Chrétien's obvious doubts about my role, he considered me a problem. His answer, to my relief, was a blunt no. He instructed me to use my own best judgment in dealing with the situation and ensuring that I was apprised of all dealings that Finkelstein had with Chrétien's team. In addition, he asked me to contact another of Chrétien's key advisors, John Rae, to tell him the general results of the meeting with Murray and Tassé.

By this time I had already accepted the possibility that a deal was in the making, so contacting Rae was at least an opportunity to make it clear that the premier still had confidence in me. The arrangement I made with Finkelstein later that afternoon was that if he was contacted by anyone like Maldoff or Goldenberg, he was free to discuss matters with them, but was also to make it clear to them that anything they discussed would be relayed to me. This request might seem dictatorial, and it undoubtedly caused Finkelstein some discomfort. But it seemed the only reasonable way to avoid hamstringing Finkelstein, and also sent a clear signal to Chrétien's team that they would have to play a reasonably open game with both me and the premier. As will be seen, however, the attempts to get around me continued throughout the first ministers' dinner.

On the day I spoke with Finkelstein, several other events stand out. The first was the publication of an article in Montreal's *Gazette* about an internal Queen's Park memo setting out a strategy to save Meech. The memo laid out a minutely detailed strategy for manipulating the media, attacking the credibility of Premier Wells, and so forth. An embarrassed David Peterson immediately disowned it and said that the low-level bureaucrat who prepared it would soon be gone. At the premier's office, all we could do was laugh, since it was obviously accurate and equally obviously not prepared by a low-level bureaucrat. (Later, reliable sources would confirm for me that it was prepared with the knowledge of Patrick Monahan.) The public outrage was not long in coming, and I hoped that it would help to undermine Peterson and the pro-Meechers on the eve of the meeting, and bolster the efforts of Premiers Wells and Filmon.

The second event was the publication of a large advertisement in all major newspapers, sponsored by the Canadians for a Unifying Constitution and obviously underwritten by the Business Council on National Issues. It urged the first ministers to sign the Accord and predicted doom if Meech failed. I can only assume that these business leaders genuinely believed that the ad could have some impact. If they did, they were even farther removed from the real world than I thought.

In any event, I had already been aware of the initiative, having spoken on the telephone late the previous day with Jack Lawrence, who was chairman of Burns Fry and one of the stalwart BCNI members spearheading Canadians for a Unifying Constitution's efforts. He had clearly been designated to alert the premier to the forthcoming advertisement.

We had an interesting and cordial exchange about other factors affecting the value of the Canadian dollar and Japanese investment decisions. I told him that in my view, it was the uncertainty itself that was most disturbing the money markets, and that the cause of this uncertainty was partly if not mainly the federal government's obvious lack of both will and direction in constitutional matters. But when Lawrence equated a first ministers' constitutional conference with a corporation's board meeting, I blanched. He suggested that if he were the lone holdout on an issue, he would inevitably assume he was

wrong and capitulate. After I reminded him there is a difference between amending a document that belongs to the *people*
of Canada and making a corporate decision, we politely
agreed to disagree. But I will always remember that conversation. With the greatest respect to Mr. Lawrence and his colleagues whose sincerity I do not at all doubt, I was not
surprised that Wells's reaction to Lawrence's comments turned
out to be the same as mine.

EIGHT

The Seven-Day Dinner

W HEN BRIAN MULRONEY announced the convening
of a first minister's dinner for Sunday, June 3, I really
did not know what to expect. The premier thought
that the meeting would carry on beyond the dinner, though
how long was uncertain. Since we had retained Neil
Finkelstein and I now believed that the premier wanted to
make a deal, I thought that discussions would probably continue for another day or two.

Whatever else I might have thought, I never expected the
meeting to go on for seven days. I was optimistic that an impasse would occur on some critical issue that would finally
force the reopening of the Accord. As a result, I brought exactly
two outfits, which certainly were put to good use every second
day of that week.

After one brief discussion with the premier on June 1, the
day after Mulroney called the meeting, I decided to gather into
some binders any relevant material for the premier's easy reference, should it prove necessary. Apart from this, I made no
other preparations for the meeting. Newfoundland's proposed
add-ons as adjusted after the two meetings with Murray were
on the table, and the premier obviously intended to use them
as his starting position. Unlike the other delegations, we had
no strategy memos, "bottom lines," or the like. The premier's
preferred approach to the constitutional debate had always
been straightforward.

Early on Sunday, June 3, I met Judy Foote, Robert Dornan, Walter Noel, Paul Dicks, and Jim Thistle at the small St. John's airport for the flight to Ottawa in an eight-seater King-Air jet. We stopped off at Deer Lake to pick up the premier, who had spent part of the weekend there. The flight took a little less than five hours, with one refuelling stop in Moncton. Without a doubt, it was one of the roughest flights I have ever been on. As we bumped our way into Ottawa's airport at about 3 p.m., Judy attempted to break the tension by saying that she hoped the premier had not told someone that he would only sign the Meech Lake Accord over his dead body.

The rest of the small Newfoundland delegation was already in Ottawa. Rosie Frey had gone ahead to ensure that all the accommodations and office arrangements were in order; as usual, she had done a superb job. Barbara Knight had also gone ahead. (I could now understand why.) Neil Finkelstein arrived from Toronto about the same time as us. Finally, there was Eugene Forsey who lived in Ottawa and who joined us for the first few critical meetings of the Newfoundland delegation.

That the Newfoundland delegation was smaller than those of other provinces was in my view an asset rather than a liability. One of the few drawbacks that we would soon notice was that the larger delegations were able to send out their extra members to give off-the-record briefings to journalists and put favourable spins on developments or non-developments throughout the week. This was especially true of the Ontario group, which appeared to include most of the cream of the Toronto legal and political-science academic establishment.

The premier called a meeting of our delegation for about 4 p.m. in a meeting room at the Chateau Laurier, which is where we were staying. Not much of substance was discussed, since everyone was so uncertain of what was going to happen next. Forsey made some of his usual perceptive and punchy comments — he said that Mulroney was selling out to Quebec nationalists — and the premier agreed. I hoped Forsey's presence might help to ensure that the premier didn't lose sight of his goals and continued his opposition to the Accord.

We also discussed Newfoundland's add-ons. Finkelstein made a few technical legal suggestions to the provision regarding the Charter, which made a bad situation perhaps a little better. I abstained from any detailed involvement in the discussion, since my general opposition to the add-on approach was clearly on the record.

My main intervention at the meeting was to suggest to the premier that he should walk out if the prime minister refused to make certain preliminary concessions — for example, to open the sessions to the public and to accept the need for substantive amendments to the Accord prior to June 23. Needless to say, the premier did not consider these suggestions to be particularly helpful and did not seriously consider them. Nevertheless, for my own peace of mind, I had to have them on the record.

The premier had worked on a draft of his opening statement on the flight to Ottawa; some further changes were now made to it. As it turned out, of course, no public opening statements were ever made.

There was also some discussion of the issue of the June 23 deadline. The premier had always taken the position that as a political if not legal matter, there was no deadline. In this connection, he shared the views of Gordon Robertson and others that because certain elements of the Accord were subject to unanimity, the three-year period did not apply to the entire package. Any deadline was just a matter of political will: if a new deal was negotiated that could be recommended to Canadians by all first ministers and that could withstand the scrutiny of meaningful public hearings, then the appropriate constitutional amendments could be proclaimed into force at the earliest possible opportunity. The apocalyptic predictions of what would happen should the June 23 deadline be missed amounted to fear-mongering of the worst kind and did much to divert the debate from the merits or demerits of the Accord.

Nevertheless, in an attempt to persuade the other first ministers to abandon the time-constraint arguments, just before leaving for Ottawa the premier had Newfoundland's justice department prepare a draft constitutional amendment that could be approved by all provincial legislatures and Parliament and implemented before June 23. This amendment would in effect have suspended the deadline and permitted discussions to continue. Needless to say, this did not suit the prime minister's brinkmanship strategy. The premier's proposal was never seriously considered except perhaps by a few provincial officials who were genuinely trying to find ways to defuse the crisis.

Throughout the week, there was never any sign of the infamous "rolling deadline" proposal announced by Lowell Murray on June 22. (With this, the federal government would argue that the Accord did not in fact expire on June 23, 1990, three years after Quebec's ratification. Rather, all that happened on that date was that Quebec's ratification would be extinguished and would have to be renewed. A similar situation would arise on the three-year anniversary of every other legislature's ratification.) The most that happened, around mid-week, was some discussion among legal advisors about the possibility of a suspended proclamation of the Accord, pending the coming into force of a companion resolution. But when it was concluded that a suspended proclamation could not be valid without appropriate resolutions of all legislatures prior to June 23, it was rapidly dropped as a serious option, since Quebec would not take any such initiative.

In this connection, a brief digression is important. After the Ottawa meeting I was informed by a reliable official from Saskatchewan that during the week in Ottawa the possibility of the same rolling deadline proposal had been raised with Mary Dawson, the FPRO's assistant deputy minister. My source was told in very clear terms that it would never work because Quebec would never agree — the proposal was contingent on the repassage of the Accord by Quebec, whose approval would be the only one that expired on June 23.

In the last few days of the debate, the same Saskatchewan official was also told to stop talking about ideas to extend the deadline "because that would give Newfoundland the excuse to postpone the vote and hold a referendum." It appears that the feds were always greatly concerned about a referendum in Newfoundland and Labrador, and rightly so, since the result would have been an unequivocal vote in favour of reopening the Accord. Brian Mulroney's subsequent "roll the dice" interview with the Globe and Mail simply brought into the open what all of us had long assumed implicitly: that the federal strategy was to exert all possible pressure on Newfoundland by escalating the threats of a post-June 23 apocalypse, while preventing a referendum.

The first ministers' dinner on Sunday night was held at the Museum of Civilization in Hull. A dinner for officials was scheduled in another room on the same floor. We were informed that only two officials from each province were entitled to the special passes to attend the dinner, and the premier chose Barbara Knight and me as the two from Newfoundland.

We headed over separately from the premier around 6 p.m. Every province was allocated a tiny office for the evening. Before the dinner began, Judy Foote and I spent some of our time watching through the windows as the other premiers arrived and made their brief two- to five-minute public remarks to the waiting media in the driveway. Certainly, there were no clues as to what was going to happen.

The dinner started at 7 p.m. *in camera*. The officials all crowded into another room for a buffet. It was clear that no other delegation had respected the two-officials limit, so Finkelstein later joined us. The other faces were all depressingly familiar, though I had only been very briefly exposed to them in November. For Ontario, Ian Scott and Patrick Monahan among others attended. Roger Tassé, Paul Tellier (clerk of the Privy Council) and Stanley Hartt (the prime minister's chief of staff), were among the prominent federal officials. Clearly the big guns were going to be playing a major role.

As Barbara Knight and I stood chatting, I noticed a number of officials talking into cellular telephones. As one attendee accurately noted, the cellular phone had now replaced the pager as the status symbol at federal-provincial conferences. But to whom could they possibly be talking? And what could they possibly be saying, since none of us had the slightest idea of what was going on inside the first ministers' room? As the week wore on, I quickly learned that these phones were a useful link between the two or three designated provincial officials outside the first ministers' inner sanctum and the hordes of other delegation members on other floors of the Conference Centre. They were also what allowed the various delegations to fuel speculation in the media by means of careful leaks, and to put the appropriate spins on the various twists and turns of the negotiations.

At 10 p.m., with the first ministers still closeted away, a bunch of officials rushed out to a room where there was a television. It seems they wanted to watch "The National" to find out what the media were saying was going on. The whole situation struck me as absurd. The dinner finally broke up close to midnight with Mulroney's announcement that a private session, essentially an extension of the dinner, would start the next day at 11 a.m. Many officials had expected that this would be how the prime minister would finesse the issue of whether a full-blown conference would be open or closed, and they were right.

We did not get a chance to find out what had gone on until we met with the premier in the Chateau Laurier just after breakfast the next day — Monday, June 4. Apparently, at the dinner, little of real substance had been discussed. There had been an obvious effort to target Wells and Filmon; the team play of McKenna and Peterson had been particularly apparent. Mulroney had made some obvious misstatements: at one point, he referred to the "mandatory delay of three years" as the reason why Meech was now unravelling. This revealed yet again his less-than-adequate familiarity with constitutional principles — there was of course nothing that mandated a delay of three years. If all provincial legislatures had approved the Accord as soon as possible after June 23, 1987, then it could have been proclaimed in force immediately thereafter. The three-year period stipulated in the Constitution was only a maximum designed to ensure that a proposed amendment affecting certain matters did not drag on counterproductively. In other words, if the requisite ratifications were not forthcoming within three years of the first, then it had to be presumed that the amendment was not capable of attracting the necessary public support to sustain its legitimacy.

During the general round-table discussion the previous night, Mulroney had pointed out that a recent Conseil du Patronat du Québec poll indicated solid support for the Accord among Quebec businesspeople, as well as increasing support for sovereignty association. Mulroney had also alluded to economic data, conveniently released that weekend, on the economic consequences of not passing the Accord — for example, an increase in Newfoundland's bond rates by several basis points above Treasury bill rates in New York, and an increase in Newfoundland's debt by $100 million because of the anticipated drop in the dollar. Incredibly, he had also pointed out that if the country broke up, Ontario and Quebec would be the twelfth and thirteenth largest economies in the world. We all choked when we heard this. As the justice minister, Paul Dicks, succinctly put it, "Brian may yet persuade Quebec to separate!"

There had been some talk of the need to address the concerns with the Accord now and of how some of the proposals put forward in Frank McKenna's companion resolution could be implemented under the general amending formula without Quebec but with the province's tacit consent. David "Mr. Reasonable" Peterson had weighed in with statements to the effect that the basics of the country were in danger and that the country could not be kept together on the basis of fear. Nevertheless, there was never any real indication from Bourassa that he was prepared to compromise. On the contrary, premiers like Joe Ghiz and John Buchanan had from time to time asserted categorically that Quebec was in no position to make concessions.

Toward the end of the dinner, Mulroney had read an excerpt from his 1983 book *Where I Stand*, in which he had set out his concern about the situation involving the Churchill Falls power contract. (This was the long-term contract that locked Newfoundland into selling power to Quebec at fire-sale prices.) The innuendo went over like a lead balloon. Perhaps Mulroney's thin skin had not recovered from the reports several weeks earlier that Wells had quoted from the same book to great effect — specifically, from the passages in which Mulroney had argued passionately in favour of an open constitutional reform process and against any special status for one province.

After the morning meeting with the Newfoundland delegation, the premier joined the other first ministers in their private meeting on the fifth floor of the Ottawa Conference Centre across the street from the Chateau Laurier. It began around 11 a.m. I sat in the officials' room across the hall and spent some time talking to British Columbia's attorney general, Bud Smith, and Gil Rémillard. There was limited access to the officials' room — only two or three passes per province. So Paul Dicks, Barbara Knight, and I used the passes, while Finkelstein and the others stayed in the small office on the main floor that had been allocated to Newfoundland.

The first ministers emerged shortly after noon. The Newfoundland delegation met with the premier for a working lunch in a meeting room at the Chateau Laurier. The premier told us that Mulroney had produced what he called a four-panel plan to direct the discussions: (1) the Meech Lake Accord would have to be ratified as it stood; (2) consideration would then be given to McKenna's companion resolution; (3) a future agenda would then be addressed that included topics like the Canada clause, Senate reform, aboriginal constitutional matters, a Code of Minority Rights, and so on; (4) finally, "clarifications" would be discussed dealing with the distinct society, the Charter, the spending power, and the role to *promote* linguistic minorities. Obviously, the concerns of Newfoundland and Manitoba were being relegated to the back burner. Equally seriously, Mulroney wanted everyone to defer the critical issues relating to the form the changes would take (that is, actual amendments to the Accord as opposed to any political declarations), when action would be taken, and the degree of certainty.

When I heard Mulroney's agenda, it was clear to me that his strategy was to grind down Wells and Filmon and then reach some agreement on, for example, potential add-ons. Only then would the issue of timing come up, and of course by that stage Wells and Filmon would be the only ones insisting that the changes be implemented before June 23. The prime minister and the rest of the first ministers would then argue that the changes could be made after the Accord was unanimously approved by June 23. At that point they would then pretend to take the high road and undermine the public support for Wells and Filmon by claiming that everyone agreed with the same changes yet Wells and Filmon were prepared to jeopardize the future of the country for a mere matter of timing.

I suggested to the premier that he should go on the offensive — in this case, insist that the "clarifications" and the issues of timing be placed on the table now, and go public if Mulroney refused. I had already argued unsuccessfully that he should refuse to attend *in camera* sessions and was not confident that this suggestion would fare any better. But I still thought it worthwhile to keep offering such strategies, if only to ensure that the premier had a range of options to consider.

The premier at least did not reject my idea out of hand and certainly seemed ill at ease with the state of discussions. A rather inconclusive debate ensued. Then, abruptly, he decided to arrange a joint meeting with Gary Filmon. This was quickly set for 1:30 p.m.

Filmon arrived on time at our Chateau Laurier meeting room, accompanied by virtually all his key advisors, from his attorney general to Wally Fox-Decent, the chair of the Manitoba Task Force on Meech Lake. I was pleased to see Bryan Schwartz among them. Schwartz was a professor of constitutional law at the University of Manitoba and was a vocal opponent of Meech — in the fall of 1987 he had written a devastating critique of the Accord titled "Fathoming Meech Lake." He was articulate and persuasive, not to mention extremely witty, and I was encouraged to find that Filmon had engaged him.

Filmon briefly outlined his objections to the Accord at the outset of the meeting. The premier's observations of the night before seemed to be true — Filmon was firm in his specific objections, and his views seemed to be based on his convictions rather than political expediency. After some rather haphazard round-table discussion — at this point there were at least fifteen people in the room — Filmon announced that when he returned to the meeting he was going to ask the other first ministers in plain terms whether they were willing to agree to amendments before June 23. At this point I believed that Filmon's position was clearer than the premier's, and that if Filmon stood firm and the premier stood with him, that question would either bring the meeting to an abrupt end or inspire actual movement towards a real compromise. I noticed that Filmon and Wells seemed to be on fairly friendly terms and expected that would help them to establish a common front.

Another, equally important development came from the meeting. The premier had decided to revise Newfoundland's add-ons slightly in order to demonstrate his good faith and bolster his and Filmon's position, which was to insist on amendments now. Newfoundland's add-ons had always included a proposal for a new preamble to the Constitution that tracked the language in Manitoba's proposal for a Canada clause. But hitherto it had not been put forward as an interpretative clause on equal footing with the distinct society clause, as was critical to Manitoba's Canada clause. At the meeting, one of Filmon's advisors suggested that our preamble be converted into an interpretative clause to bring it closer into line with the Manitoba proposal. Wells agreed to this.

My immediate reaction was positive. I thought the change would help to link the two provinces and strengthen their resistance to the pro-Meechers' strategy, which was to divide Manitoba and Newfoundland. More specifically, I believed that the pro-Meech forces wanted to isolate Filmon on the issue of the Canada clause, which had not been a critical component of Newfoundland's position; and then isolate Wells on the issue of special legislative status, which was not a concern of Manitoba; and then shuffle off the other mutual Newfoundland/Manitoba concerns like Senate reform to a second round, or the Charter to a mere political declaration.

When the first ministers reconvened around 3 p.m. in their fifth-floor room, it was announced that each could be joined by his province's attorney general. Paul Dicks joined the premier. About thirty minutes later, all of the attorneys general were asked to leave, and they joined the officials in the room across the hall. I was impatient, thinking that Filmon was finally going to put his question to the other first ministers. Unfortunately, it appears that whatever Filmon said, the issue of the timing of amendments was deferred yet again. I was tremendously disappointed — I could not believe that *both* Filmon and Wells could be so easily manipulated by Mulroney. The optimism I had carried from the lunch meeting quickly vanished.

After almost an hour, the attorneys general returned to the meeting, which then dragged on until about 8 p.m. Apparently, the discussion centred on the issue of Senate reform and how to make the unanimity rule more acceptable by establishing that a province's veto could be overridden by a mandatory referendum. In addition, the "Ghiz/Pickersgill ass-kicker" proposal was put on the table. Jack Pickersgill had raised the proposal in an open editorial in the *Ottawa Citizen* that day, and Ghiz now put it forward. (Who gave it such a tasteless label is anyone's guess.) The idea was that intensive negotiations on Senate reform would continue until 1992, at which time, if there was no agreement, an automatic redistribution of seats would take place to enhance the representation of small provinces, and the Senate would retain its same plenary powers. The underlying assumption was that the prospect of an automatic redistribution would galvanize recalcitrant provinces into seeking an early agreement.

The first ministers' meeting broke up inconclusively with an agreement simply to reconvene the next morning. That evening marked the start of what was to become a regular routine whenever the first ministers made the trek through the entrance of the Conference Centre across to either the Chateau

Laurier or the Westin Hotel. Every time meetings broke up, mobs of reporters and photographers would line both sides of the sidewalk crushed behind metal gates and shout questions at each passing premier. All the regulars were there, including Don Newman of CBC Newsworld and Wendy Mesley of *The National*. I couldn't get over the amount of money and time the media were obviously investing in covering the meetings, all in the hope of catching a rushed response in a haphazard way from the first ministers.

From time to time, however, premiers would pause at a microphone to provide an impromptu press conference. After Monday's meeting, Frank McKenna stopped to announce that New Brunswick now endorsed the Meech Lake Accord. Given that he had said as much when he introduced the companion resolution, this was a non-event if I ever saw one. As my cynicism mounted, I presumed that he was trying to put out at least some "good news" at the end of the day and to pretend that there was some "momentum" for agreement. Certainly, as far as I could tell, Premier Wells considered McKenna's announcement insignificant.

That evening Wells hosted an impromptu dinner in his suite for the other premiers, all of whom attended except McKenna. Apparently it was the Atlantic premiers' idea. I was somewhat bemused by the dinner; given the relaxed atmosphere, I had to believe that a deal might well be worked out.

There was little to be done at the officials' level, so I spent the evening returning calls to some reporters who wanted Newfoundland's position to be explained or clarified. Earlier that day Judy Foote and I had become aware that Norman Spector and other officials were giving off-the-record briefings and putting a favourable spin on events. Judy thought I should assist her in talking to the various reporters who were calling to ask for alternative explanations and predictions.

I agreed, but it was always an exhausting uphill battle. During one conversation, an *Ottawa Citizen* reporter asked me if the premier would now moderate his position on special legislative status, given that most of the premiers were in agreement on the issue. I was surprised, to say the least, and responded that to my knowledge the issue of special legislative status was still very much under discussion. When I questioned him on this point, he told me that Norman Spector had suggested earlier that day that this issue had been resolved.

In another conversation, a *Globe and Mail* financial reporter quizzed me about Newfoundland's response to the predictions that if Meech failed, economic catastrophe would follow. I suggested in exasperation that he should also quiz the PMO types about what sort of back-up plan they had, since the uncertainty about whether the feds *had* a back-up plan was as unsettling to the financial markets as the possibility that the Accord might fail. The reporter agreed, but added that he could never get any PMO types to comment. I suggested that he write an article about the fact that they refused to comment. He never did.

On Tuesday, June 5, the Newfoundland delegation met for what was to be a regular early-morning breakfast meeting in the premier's suite. Wells seemed relaxed and announced that he planned to present to the other premiers his absolute irreducible minimum of changes to the Accord. He then said that he wanted to set out three essential areas of add-ons: the first to deal with concerns relating to the Charter and special legislative status arising from the distinct society clause; the second to involve a sunset clause on the veto over Senate reform; and the third to mitigate the restrictions on the federal spending power. I immediately voiced my concern that this would involve dropping the preamble proposal, which I saw as our critical link with Manitoba's position. The premier listened politely, but made it clear that he did not consider the link important, and so I resigned myself to his direction. For the first time, I was really frustrated that the premier did not think more strategically and, for example, see the advantage of the Manitoba link, and was not sufficiently on guard against manipulation. As usual, I still held out hope that even his irreducible minimum would prove unacceptable and that the Accord would eventually be reopened, but I had also resigned myself to the fact that if the others were prepared to move on these issues, there would be a compromise — which is precisely why Neil Finkelstein was there. It was obvious that the premier was under enormous pressure to approve the Accord in its present version, and though I was sympathetic, I was also disappointed that the politics of manipulation might soon win out over principle.

The first ministers reconvened around 10 a.m., and I headed up to the officials' room in the small elevator with Newfoundland MHA Walter Noel, who had taken one of the

floating passes. Coincidentally, we ended up sharing the elevator with Gil Rémillard and Robert Bourassa. We exchanged
small talk and then Rémillard, to my astonishment, asked us
whether we would all be in the same country tomorrow. Noel
and I promptly replied yes, at which point both Rémillard and
Bourassa shook their heads and Bourassa mumbled, "I think
not." I can only assume that this was all part of a conscious
strategy to escalate the pressure. But what a method!

The first ministers' meeting went on *in camera* virtually
non-stop through lunch until early afternoon. I spent most of
the time talking to other officials on the fifth floor. In the afternoon, the Saskatchewan delegation's draft of a Canada clause
began to circulate on photocopied sheets. This provided the
occasion for the first structured discussions among officials.
Up to this point, we all had mainly engaged in small talk.

To accommodate all of the officials' meetings, the rule
about restricted access to the fifth floor had apparently been
lifted. This meant that most of the Manitoba and Newfoundland delegates were able to crowd into a small fifth-floor room
to examine the draft together. This was in my view a critical
meeting because we reached the conclusion that Newfoundland's concerns about special legislative status could be
addressed just as well through a modification of a sub-clause
in the Canada clause that mentioned the principle of the equality of the provinces. I saw this as potentially an excellent way
to ensure that Newfoundland could support Manitoba's
Canada clause, even though it was not exactly part of our irreducible minimum. From then on, at every opportunity, I put
forward the argument for the Canada clause option. I believe
this played an important role in shaking up, at least temporarily, the feds' carefully laid out plans to isolate Manitoba
on the Canada clause.

A few minutes after the meeting began, both Wells and Filmon joined us and announced that we would divide into two
groups. Vic Taves of Manitoba, Jim Thistle, the deputy minister
of justice, and I would join Roger Tassé to discuss Newfoundland's proposed add-ons to deal with the Charter and the
special legislative status. At the same time, Neil Finkelstein
would join a larger meeting of officials from all the other provinces to discuss the Canada clause. The premiers then returned to their *in camera* session. I don't know how it was
decided that Newfoundland's concerns about the distinct

society clause should be isolated in a bilateral meeting, but I was convinced that manipulation was underway to keep Manitoba and Newfoundland apart.

At my meeting, Tassé put forward the now-familiar federal position that the distinct society clause did not create a special legislative status, but that Ottawa might be prepared to examine a new subsection similar to the Chrétien proposal that he had discussed with Wells in St. John's. In the end, the meeting was inconclusive and frustrating, and not only because of Tassé's position. I was favourably impressed with Taves, who had obviously been instructed to support whatever position Newfoundland took. I was shocked, however, when our own deputy minister began suggesting amendments that weakened the already minimalist Newfoundland position. Admittedly, it was unfortunate that Thistle had not been more fully briefed on the background leading to the draft; even so, I found it incredible that he would directly contradict me on several points. I then remembered that he had from the beginning disagreed with the premier's interpretation of the distinct society clause, and that he had been part of Brian Peckford's team during the original Meech Lake negotiations. Clearly, his views had not changed.

Fortunately, just before we reached an explosion point — I was about to ask Thistle to step outside the room for a moment so I could speak to him in private — the first ministers concluded their evening session. It was about 7 p.m. Both officials' meetings were then interrupted so that we could confer with our respective premiers. While the deputy minister and Neil Finkelstein were in one of the Conference Centre rooms, I was able to describe to Wells the nature of the dispute in the Tassé meeting without expressly mentioning the deputy minister. As I expected, the premier indicated that he disagreed with Thistle's position. He then instructed us that if there was ever any disagreement among Newfoundland officials, we were immediately to break off any meeting and consult with him to resolve the situation before the meeting proceeded. This direction seemed entirely sensible to me.

The Tassé meeting resumed. Finkelstein now joined Taves, the deputy, and me, since his meeting on the Canada clause had wound up inconclusively. Finkelstein was able to recover any ground that we might have lost. By midnight we too wound up rather inconclusively, with Newfoundland's add-ons still on the table in more or less the same condition. Tassé emphasized again and again how difficult it would be for Quebec to accept anything and that the Charter add-on would be difficult enough, never mind any add-on relating to the special legislative status. That was the frustrating theme of the entire week — there was never really any objective, rational discussion of the merits of any proposal or concern — just "What is acceptable to Quebec?" To which the answer was invariably, "Nothing that would involve any amendment to the Accord prior to June 23."

NINE

Caught in the Vortex

OUR BREAKFAST MEETING on Wednesday, June 6, gave us little indication of how long the ordeal was going to last. The premier simply relayed some of the details of the rather desultory talks on Senate reform and other matters. Meanwhile, Robert Bourassa was refusing to discuss anything other than the topics for the second round. Wells seemed discouraged.

What surprised me the most at this stage was how much success the pro-Meech forces were having in pressuring Wells to compromise. Like everyone around him, he knew how massive his public support was, and he must have known that if he just said "enough is enough" and walked out, this support would increase. Yet clearly, the constant reminders in the first ministers' meetings that he would be responsible for killing Meech and possibly destroying Canada were successfully getting to him — to the extent, at least, that he felt compelled to soldier on in discussions that could only lead to more concessions. I wasn't prepared for this disturbing dimension to the debate. Since I wasn't able to witness the pressure tactics being used against him in the closed meetings, I found it impossible to assess their impact on the premier.

That morning during a break, Wells and Filmon emerged briefly from the closed meeting to discuss the possibility of a delayed proclamation of the Accord pending the approval of a companion resolution. Wells seemed tense and a little on edge. This time we all met in the office of the Manitoba delegation on the main floor. The best legal advice from both Finkelstein and the Manitoba lawyers was that even this would require eleven new resolutions prior to June 23, which was once more out of the question for Quebec. I felt depressed: both men were now desperately seeking a way to "save the Accord" and accommodate the others. It was clear to me that they were being gradually forced to retreat, and that once they abandoned their insistence that the Accord be changed before it came into force, capitulation was just a matter of time.

During a brief meeting with the premier around noon in Newfoundland's ground-floor office, Sharon Carstairs made an appearance. The premier suggested that she come back and speak to me in the afternoon. When she returned, Finkelstein and I explained to her the stage the talks were at, the Newfoundland add-ons, the debate on Manitoba's Canada clause, and so on. Carstairs replied that it was important for her to know exactly what Newfoundland's position was at any given point, since she had told Filmon that she would stick with Wells, whose position would in effect govern the extent of her support for Filmon. She then explained that she had been "informed" that Wells only supported a new preamble to the Constitution, not the full-blown interpretative Canada clause that Manitoba wanted.

I was surprised and quickly explained that while it was true that Newfoundland's add-ons involved a new preamble, this was only one of several add-ons. I then explained that Newfoundland was fully prepared to support Manitoba's Canada clause and indeed use it to accommodate our add-on regarding special legislative status. It was obvious to me what was happening: Carstairs's "informers" were trying to persuade her that Wells was not prepared to hold out for the Canada clause, in which case she would presumably "stick with Wells" and undermine Filmon's commitment to a Canada clause. Many pro-Meech strategists believed that this Canada clause commitment was the biggest obstacle to overcome vis-à-vis Manitoba and that once they had overcome it, they could focus exclusively on grinding down Wells.

At this stage, I was not certain who Carstairs was listening to, but I suspected it was Jean Chrétien and his advisors. Sure enough, I soon discovered that they were camped out in the Chateau Laurier. Shortly after Carstairs left, Finkelstein went back into a meeting to discuss the Canada clause. A message was relayed to me on the fifth floor from our office that Carstairs had called looking for Finkelstein, and I was asked to return the call.

I did, and Carstairs rather uncomfortably told me that she was not really the person who wanted to speak to Finkelstein; it was Eric Maldoff. I bluntly replied that Finkelstein had already made arrangements with me regarding his contact with Maldoff and others and that Maldoff could relay his message to Finkelstein through me. Carstairs was clearly aware of the situation and quickly hung up without putting Maldoff on. I now realized that we would have a second front to deal with.

I sent the premier a note about the probable Carstairs-Maldoff-Chrétien-Hartt pipeline. He emerged to express his concerns about being used in some behind-the-scenes way. I then arranged to join a new meeting of some officials, which the premier had initiated, to discuss in general terms the concerns of Newfoundland and Manitoba and the appropriate add-ons.

About that time, David Peterson came out of the meeting room with a draft of a preamble, which had emerged from somewhere, and sat down at a round table in the open lounge area to talk about it with the Quebec officials. It was one of the weakest versions I had yet seen, and it was clear that the Quebec officials were not the slightest bit interested. This did not bode well for the much stronger Canada clause and confirmed most people's assumptions — that Quebec was not prepared to budge one inch.

By now the various pieces of paper floating around the meetings were creating chaos. Canada clauses and preambles would emerge virtually out of thin air, and officials would casually discuss issues working from different drafts. At one point, I began noting the date and time of receipt of any piece of paper in order to try to regulate the chaos. I have since been told by several very experienced intergovernmental officials that without a doubt this was the most disorganized and disconnected conference they had ever attended.

That afternoon I had my first direct run-in with Ontario's attorney general, Ian Scott. The premier and Filmon had decided that a small meeting of selected officials should be held that evening to discuss the distinct society clause. The premier had expressly asked that constitutional expert and Ontario official Peter Hogg be invited to attend. (A legal opinion Hogg had written for the Ontario government had concluded that no special legislative status was created by this clause.)

I cannot remember quite how it came about, but Scott was present at one of the many spontaneous corridor meetings among officials. When he learned of the more formal meeting that Filmon and Wells had arranged, he stated abruptly that Patrick Monahan would also attend. (Neither he nor Monahan had been invited.) I replied equally abruptly that since this was a restricted meeting, I would have to ask the premier for instructions. As I expected, the premier indicated that this was not to be a full-scale officials' meeting and that only Hogg was invited. When I relayed this to Scott, he was affronted. Finally, I told him that my instructions came from Wells and that he was free to consult Peterson. Ultimately, he did just that. Peterson in turn spoke to Wells. In the end, both he and Monahan attended the meeting, as did Roger Tassé and Mary Dawson. Apparently, the word went out that this meeting was the place to be, and it grew to a rather unwieldy size of some fifteen or so officials.

The discussion ended in an inconclusive exchange of legal views regarding the impact of the distinct society clause. Finkelstein, Scott, and Hogg were the main participants. Most interesting from my perspective was the presence of three key advisors from Quebec — André Tremblay, Jean K. Samson, and Benoit Morin. These three participated constructively in the exchange and admitted that the clause would of course have some substantive effect, though in their view only a minimal one.

The premier arrived around 10:30 p.m., after the break-up of the first ministers' meeting, but stayed only briefly and did not really join in. He encouraged everyone to keep talking and then headed back to the hotel. The meeting then dissolved. Finkelstein continued a private meeting with Tremblay about how to accommodate Newfoundland's proposed add-on to the distinct society clause. He seemed to think that there was some way of drafting it that would satisfy Quebec, and Tremblay professed interest. I was sceptical but of course did not interfere. Instead, I finished off some work at the office. Shortly after midnight, Finkelstein came down to the office, and he and I walked back to the Chateau Laurier together. As we entered the lobby, out of the blue appeared Eric Maldoff and

Eddie Goldenberg, who looked very surprised to see me. The second front had arrived.

It was clear that Maldoff, Goldenberg, and then John Rae — who emerged from the elevator a few minutes later — were hoping to meet Finkelstein alone. Although I have no doubt that Finkelstein would have honoured our arrangement and spoken to me after, I also have no doubt that he would have joined some old friends for a drink. Obviously, the aim of the Chrétien team was to use him as a direct route to the premier.

My presence spoiled whatever had been in the works at that moment. Finkelstein, who was clearly uncomfortable, said hello and good night to them. As we walked to our rooms, which were on the same floor of the Chateau, I apologized to Finkelstein for placing him in an awkward position. I believe he understood.

At Thursday's breakfast meeting, I was exhausted. As the premier summarized Wednesday's meetings, it seemed to me the wheels were spinning. None of the pro-Meech premiers had changed their positions, and neither had the prime minister. Not only was Bourassa insisting on only discussing topics for the second round, but both he and Mulroney were back to the old fallacious arguments: Quebec already had an effective veto over Senate reform, so why the concern? (In fact, their argument was legally wrong and had already been decisively rejected in a memorandum by Manitoba's constitutional expert, Bryan Schwartz, some weeks earlier.)

All that had really been discussed the previous day were various components of McKenna's companion resolution; the critical issues of timing and certainty were sidestepped yet again. Once more, my only thought was that the premier and Filmon must threaten and then, if necessary, carry out the threat to walk out and go public, if Mulroney continued to refuse to permit an open meeting and to settle the issues of the timing and certainty of any amendments. I felt that the premier had already compromised far too much and was losing his perspective after three exhausting days of inconclusive meetings. I told him that, but he was still reluctant to walk out, believing that further discussions were still worthwhile.

Finkelstein mentioned that he and Tremblay had kept trying the evening before to find common ground on an add-on to the distinct society clause and that Tremblay had called him early in the morning to discuss a variation on Newfoundland's proposal that he had formulated overnight. Wells encouraged him to keep the discussions going. So once the first ministers went into their private morning session, Finkelstein and I met Tremblay in the fifth-floor lounge and discussed Tremblay's variation. Not surprisingly, it would have simply confirmed the special legislative status by stating explicitly that under the distinct society clause Quebec could legislate in respect of a distinct characteristic not shared by other provinces — that is, its francophone majority.

I was most surprised, however, to hear Finkelstein say that he thought it might be acceptable to the premier. Knowing the premier's views on special status, I thought the premier could not possibly go along with it. Moreover, Tremblay had the honesty to admit that this was only his own proposal and that Quebec could never officially accept it as an amendment to the Accord. At most, it could be set out in a legal opinion of some sort that Quebec would not sign and that would have little if any legal weight in the courts. This statement showed how astonishingly inflexible Quebec was, and further convinced me that Quebec's delegation, at least, no longer had the slightest interest in saving the Accord.

Our meeting with Tremblay broke up on the understanding that his proposal would be put to the premier when he came out of the first ministers' meeting. Finkelstein and I then discussed the proposal: he thought it would actually limit the application of the distinct society clause; I thought that the powers it gave Quebec to promote its francophone majority could extend to virtually any action taken by the Quebec government.

In further corridor discussions with Ontario and Manitoba officials, I was relieved to find that Manitoba's advisors, including Vic Taves, shared my view that Tremblay's proposal would in fact underline Quebec's special legislative status. Finkelstein and I then wrote a brief memo for the premier setting out the pros and cons of the proposal. I inserted my recommendation that it was more worthwhile at this stage to drop the idea of a separate clarification of the distinct society clause altogether and to pursue the Canada clause option for dealing with Newfoundland's concerns about special legislative status. Once more I was determined to ensure that Newfoundland would support Manitoba's Canada clause.

Later in the morning, when I was talking to the premier and several Manitoba officials in the corridor outside the inner sanctum, Gary Filmon suddenly emerged and joined us. I took the opportunity to remind them all that Newfoundland's concerns could be dealt with through the Canada clause and to ask outright what was happening to the clause in the first ministers' meeting. As I expected, Filmon replied that it was not yet seriously "on the table." This thoroughly discouraged me, but I hoped that jogging their thoughts in the area might be helpful.

The premiers worked through lunch. Then, in the early afternoon, the premier suddenly reappeared to call a meeting of Manitoba's legal advisors, the three Manitoba party leaders, Finkelstein, me, and by invitation, Roger Tassé and Peter Hogg.*

While we waited for the Manitoba opposition leaders to arrive, I had a few moments with the premier and passed on Finkelstein's and my memo on the Tremblay proposal. He skimmed it, but made no comment on its substance. We all then congregated in a spare room on a lower floor for the meeting.

The Manitoba party leaders and the premier first had a private session while the rest of us sat in the corridor. After we joined them, everyone proceeded through a fairly clear-cut agenda. We started with the feds' add-on proposal to the distinct society clause — the one that had originally been put forward by Tassé in May and that had earlier resurfaced in the Maldoff document. The premier asked what the difference in legal impact would be between putting it in a mere political declaration by first ministers and making it an express amendment to the Accord or other constitutional provision. Tassé and Hogg, among others, confirmed that a political declaration would carry at most "some weight" in the courts, certainly less weight than an actual amendment.

We then moved ahead to the Newfoundland add-on dealing with the special legislative status created by the distinct society clause. Tassé and Hogg both repeated their well-known

---

* Some Manitoba officials were always taken aback when the premier consulted Peter Hogg from time to time, since he was officially part of the Ontario delegation and inevitably suspect. The premier was not "caving in"; rather, he genuinely respected Hogg's ability to give objective constitutional advice, as did I.

views that of course the add-on was not necessary since Quebec did not get any special powers, but they also added that Tremblay's variation of this add-on could at least be considered for a political declaration. The Manitoba advisors then stated their concern, which I shared, that Tremblay's reference to Quebec legislating to promote its francophone majority could extend to almost anything and would actually confirm the special legislative status.

Again, we just moved on, but this time to the Canada clause, which was the interpretative clause that would set out the fundamental characteristics of Canada. Here, fortunately, the premier himself raised the possibility that concerns about the special legislative status could be addressed in the Canada clause subsection involving the principle of the equality of the provinces. Tassé began to look distinctly uncomfortable as he realized what was going on. The premier then asked Hogg directly whether the Canada clause option would accomplish the same end as the Tremblay clause in eliminating any special legislative status. Hogg advised him that it would. I heaved a sigh of relief — this provided us with a great tactical advantage, as was obvious immediately from Tassé's agitation. He began to argue that the principle of equality of the provinces was already in the preamble to the Meech Lake Accord and that therefore there was no need to put it in again in the Canada clause. At one point he even rose from his seat and went around the table to point out the preamble reference for Filmon. Of course, he did not add that this preambular reference was of zero legal significance, and that the reference in the Canada clause would have much more legal weight. I hoped that both the premier and Filmon, as well as Sharon Carstairs and Gary Doer, could sense what was happening. Tassé was now worried that Manitoba and Newfoundland would form a common front, linking the former's Canada clause with the latter's special status concerns. This of course would have frustrated the federal strategy, which was to isolate the two provinces from each other.

At the end of the meeting, the other details of the Canada clause were discussed, and Tassé made the now-standard argument that it was not necessary to have the Canada clause in interpretative form like the distinct society clause. Finkelstein and the Manitoba officials set out the opposite case — that the two clauses should be similar. Tassé knew the Quebec delegation did not want to dilute the special status of the distinct society clause by giving the Canada clause equal weight. This was yet another example of extraordinary narrow-mindedness.

After the meeting, all of the legal advisors left the political leaders alone again. This was around 4 p.m. Twenty minutes later, Bourassa suddenly appeared with Tassé and entered the room alone. (Tassé wanted to join him but it was decided that the meeting would be for politicians only.) Bourassa emerged some fifteen minutes later and disappeared. The others emerged shortly after.

It was now 5 p.m. The premier, Finkelstein, and I returned to the fifth floor for a brief meeting with the other Newfoundland officials. The premier now indicated that he and Filmon had agreed on a joint "bottom line." I was disturbed to learn that the first element would be a mere political declaration regarding the impact of the distinct society clause on the Charter — a major concession in my view and unwarranted since no one else seemed to be making any concessions. But I was too numb at this point to make a full-scale protest, and only voiced my surprise. The remaining joint bottom line included the following provisions: a Canada clause with the all-important equality-of-provinces sub-clause; something on Senate reform such as the Ghiz-Pickersgill proposal; and a provision, as yet unspecified, to deal with the issues related to the federal spending power. These provisions were more encouraging, because they signalled that Newfoundland would stick with Manitoba on the Canada clause. Perhaps this show of solidarity would force the others to revise their "isolate and grind down" strategy.

The premier then went back into the private meetings, and we returned to the officials' room for several hours of tense waiting. Rumours soon began to fly that shouting had been heard, that someone was about to walk out, and so on. The cellular telephones were going wild.

About 9 p.m., the premier's executive assistant came up from our delegation office and handed us a one-line press release that had just been issued by the Quebec delegation. It stated bluntly that the Quebec premier had announced that he would no longer participate in any further discussion of the distinct society clause. Incredibly, Bourassa was still in the conference room with the other first ministers and had not informed them of the statement, as we subsequently learned from the premier, to whom we immediately sent a copy.

Obviously, whatever Robert Bourassa was saying in the private sessions, the political heat from the PQ opposition in Quebec was beginning to tell on him. Jacques Parizeau, the PQ leader, had performed effectively at a press conference the day before, and most speculation among officials on Thursday morning focused on how much longer Bourassa could politically afford to stay locked up, and whether *he* would walk before Filmon or Wells.

As Patrick Monahan set out in his recent account of the Meech debate, Ontario's Ian Scott had decided that Wells and Filmon were not getting the message that Meech had to pass without changes and that a "reality check" was needed to jolt them. He discussed this with the Quebec delegation which undoubtedly contributed to the decision to issue a press release. It would be difficult to find a more arrogant and insensitive initiative.

Scott's involvement certainly fits with an event that occurred a few minutes later as the first ministers' meeting was breaking up with considerable disarray and acrimony. Just before the premier emerged, while Finkelstein and I were waiting in the corridor, he marched over and shouted at us, "You have taken Canada apart. You have! You have!" I had always known that Scott was an effective trial lawyer, but in these circumstances the theatrics were excessive. Moreover, neither Finkelstein nor I had a clue about what had happened. At that moment, the premier arrived, looking tense, and we all quickly walked over to his room in the Chateau for a meeting.

Apparently, Wells had presented the other premiers with the joint Manitoba/Newfoundland bottom line, and Bourassa and Peterson had blown up and accused him of trying to break up Canada. Ghiz also joined the harangue. For some reason, they had expected this presentation to be much milder, which astounded me, since from my perspective Newfoundland's position was now pared to the bone.

I returned to my room close to midnight. But I was not to have much rest, since the second front was getting back to work, in the person this time of Brian Tobin, the Newfoundland MP who was chairman of the federal Liberal caucus and Chrétien's "agent" during the constitutional talks. Tobin had been trying to call the premier to warn him that the federal spin doctors were out trying to pin the blame on the nasty Liberals and that they were furiously spreading stories — for example, that somehow Sharon Carstairs was responsible for the blow-up of the first ministers' meeting that night.

My first reaction was how absurd, and that the situation could easily be spun back to reality by an explanatory statement the next day by the premier, which I would definitely discuss with him at the next day's breakfast meeting. I told myself that Tobin was likely worried that his boss was failing to "deliver" Carstairs and Wells, and that the feds were preparing to cut the lines of communication and begin a full-scale attack on Chrétien, which would heighten the present divisions within the Liberal Party. Tobin continued to play an active role as Chrétien's agent throughout the week as well as during the days leading to the June 23 deadline. Mainly, this would involve pressuring individual Newfoundland MHAs to support the Accord in the free vote and creating deliberately false spins in Ottawa by saying that the premier actually wanted the Accord to pass.

TEN

Master Manipulators
at Work

MY FEARS ABOUT THE SECOND front were realized on Friday morning. I arrived at the premier's room for the breakfast meeting to find television cameras and reporters camped outside. The premier was already meeting with Neil Finkelstein, Eddie Goldenberg, Eric Maldoff, and Sharon Carstairs. I did not join the meeting, but waited in the dining room with the other members of the Newfoundland delegation.

After they left, the premier did not speak to me about what had transpired. Finkelstein later explained that he had received an anxious phone call from Maldoff and Goldenberg at 6:45 a.m. asking for an urgent meeting with the premier. I have subsequently learned that Chrétien's people supposedly wanted to warn Wells of federal "spins" that claimed the premier was emotionally unstable. (Apparently there had been some tense exchanges among Wells and several other premiers the evening before, when Wells presented the joint Newfound-land/Manitoba position. Several premiers reportedly accused Wells of trying to break up Canada.) Presumably, they also wanted to talk about Tobin's concerns that Mulroney would attempt to blame the Liberals.

Given that Chrétien's people were desperately hoping for a deal and that they considered me a block to the premier, I could only view their visit as manipulative. This was confirmed when I learned the following week that back in Winnipeg, Sharon Carstairs was confiding in friends that the premier had had a nervous breakdown on the Thursday evening. This rumour was scurrilous, but it leads one to believe that during the Ottawa meetings Carstairs and company were actually heightening the effect of the federal spins in order to undermine Wells and conclude an agreement.

Over breakfast the premier was tense and very short-tempered and announced that he was now totally frustrated and was going to call a press conference to explain exactly what was going on, to indicate how far Newfoundland and Manitoba had compromised and how intransigent everyone else was. Judy Foote agreed with the idea, but advised the premier not to inform the other premiers first; otherwise, as she was now fully aware, the spin doctors would be out immediately to pre-empt or bury his statements.

Finkelstein and I were instructed to draw up a brief paper indicating the evolution of Newfoundland's position up to the present time. We did this in the Newfoundland office after the first ministers began their private session. (Bourassa remained at the hotel, as was consistent with his press release.) Only at this point did Finkelstein point out that at the morning meeting with Goldenberg, Maldoff, and Carstairs, the premier had given ground even on the bare-bones bottom line of the previous evening. More specifically, he had apparently suggested that he could accept a political declaration not only on the Charter concern about the distinct society clause, but also on the special legislative status. In other words, the Canada clause, our link to Manitoba, had now been dropped from Newfoundland's list.

When I heard this concession, I exploded at Finkelstein and the others in the office, who happened to include Eugene Forsey. I told Finkelstein that I was absolutely certain that within ten minutes of the meeting, the premier's views would have been in Stanley Hartt's hands via Chrétien's people and must even now be on the table in some form in front of the first ministers. Filmon's resolve that the Canada clause must be implemented by June 23 would now be undermined, since Carstairs would of course "stick with Wells" and abandon her support for Filmon, at least with respect to the Canada clause.

Without a doubt, this was the most upsetting moment of that entire ordeal. What bothered me the most was not the prospect of an agreement, to which I was already resigned, but the unfair manipulation by the premier's fellow Liberals, who were now deliberately undermining the premier's negotiating strength and forcing him to capitulate rather than seek a compromise.

But still more upsetting news was on the way. Eugene Forsey sadly submitted his resignation from the delegation so that he could be free to criticize the entire process and whatever product might emerge. I could not blame him — he too had observed the steady erosion of Newfoundland's position and could not accept what was happening. Although he had not been at many of our meetings, he had dropped by the office regularly every day and knew what was happening. Just the day before, I had been angered to learn that after Rosie and I had arranged a pass for him to the fifth-floor officials' room, federal government bureaucrats had refused him access. A more disgraceful and disrespectful situation would be hard to imagine.

I sent Forsey's handwritten letter of resignation to the premier, who apparently read it out to the other first ministers and told them that it was one of the saddest things that he had ever received. He relayed his regrets by speaking personally to Forsey when he emerged for a brief lunch break.

Meanwhile, the material that Finkelstein and I had put together was complete, and Judy and I began to speculate about when the premier might call the press conference. However, it transpired that against Judy's advice, but consistent with his openness, the premier had announced his intentions to the other first ministers. Mulroney of course pressed him to defer the conference, not to jump prematurely, and so on. The conference never took place.

Private meetings continued all afternoon and into the evening, with various premiers, including Wells, emerging from time to time to ask advice about this or that proposal. Although no one had any idea how close an agreement might be, I was now resigned to the fact that something would soon emerge. Judy, Robert Dornan, and I were now concerned mainly about ensuring that at the very least the premier respected his numerous assertions that he would never sign a document behind closed doors without first allowing the people of Newfoundland and Labrador to have their say.

During the last few hours before the tentative deal was reached — which happened about 8 p.m. — I finally had an opportunity to speak more informally with some of Gary Filmon's advisors. In at least some cases, their opposition to Meech ran as deep as mine. They were as upset as I was to see their premier making compromises while the pro-Meech forces dug in. Up to the moment the deal was announced, I never gave up hope that something might happen to make Filmon and Wells call a halt to the process. I certainly never expected that the jolt, at least where Wells was concerned, would come *after* a tentative deal had been reached.

I also had some long conversations with Newfoundland's justice minister, Paul Dicks. As it turned out, his views on the substance of the Accord often coincided with mine. He was fully aware of the manipulation that was going on and the tactics being used. He also had a valuable political perspective on how all this was playing to the public back home. He was equally aware of the Chrétien/Goldenberg/Maldoff team's involvement, and I told him what I thought of their unacceptable tactics and unnecessary involvement. At one point in the afternoon, he was called over for a meeting with Brian Tobin, Eric Maldoff, and Eddie Goldenberg in the Chateau and given the now-familiar message: the Accord is bad but rejecting it now would be worse and it was time to hold our noses and jump. I joked with him, saying he should tell them he first had to check with Coyne. It would have been worth saying just for the expression on their faces.

I understand that Dicks was later classified as a "Chrétien person" under Tobin's influence who would likely vote in favour of the Accord in the free vote. But for anyone who listened to Dicks's opening speech in the debate, in which he condemned Meech as an example of appeasement à la Munich, it is beyond comprehension that he would have voted in favour of the Accord. To the extent that such rumours were being circulated by Tobin and others, this was a further example of the manipulation and spins that obscured the final days of the debate.

Around 8 p.m. the premiers emerged and joined the mob in the officials' room. The word quickly spread that there was a tentative deal. As expected, it involved the accepting of Meech without amendments, as well as a companion resolution and future talks. Wells looked exhausted, and I was concerned that it was simply impossible now for him to assess how much he had conceded. By this time I was so worn out I could barely distinguish one day from the next; as the premier said later that night, it was like being caught up in a vortex from which you could not escape. He confirmed that there was an agreement and then at one point turned to me and said, "I know you won't like it, Debbie." He was definitely not happy, but he seemed resigned and relieved that the ordeal was over.

While we were still in the fifth-floor room, the premier explained that he had been prepared to walk out around 5 p.m. and call his press conference, when suddenly David Peterson emerged with "the big concession": Ontario would give up six of its twenty-four Senate seats for redistribution to the less populous provinces as part of the Ghiz-Pickersgill Senate reform proposal while Quebec would keep its present twenty-four seats. Wells was impressed, and an agreement was then worked out. I readily admit that in the isolated, pressure-cooker atmosphere of the meeting, this proposal must have seemed astounding. But in the hard light of day, it represented little real progress toward the goal of a Triple-E Senate and meaningful Senate reform. I was amazed at how the dynamics of the meeting could have led the premier to think that this was an impressive initiative.

In addition, Mulroney apparently agreed to establish a joint federal-provincial fisheries management board as part of the deal on McKenna's companion resolution. (This resolution would have eliminated the mandatory annual first ministers' conferences on fisheries jurisdiction.) This board was highly desirable from Newfoundland's perspective, and something that Nova Scotia adamantly opposed, since its fishing rights would inevitably be curtailed in favour of Newfoundland's. As the premier told us about it, we could see an upset John Buchanan conferring anxiously with his officials in another corner of the officials' room. Consistent with his integrity on constitutional matters, Wells insisted that this non-constitutional issue not be viewed as in any way a *quid pro quo* for his agreement to Meech. He refused to accept a letter stating formally that Mulroney had made the offer and agreed that the board should not be mentioned as part of any final package. (Of course, after the Accord's failure, Mulroney went back to stonewalling on the issue. The joint management board still has not seen the light of day.)

The one encouraging point was that the premier had insisted that he would have to get approval from the people of Newfoundland and Labrador in some way before the Accord could be ratified. If he decided to recommend it, however, it would undoubtedly be approved. I am sure the other first ministers were counting on this.

After standing around in the fifth-floor officials' room for about twenty minutes, the premier came down to the office for a quiet thirty minutes alone with Judy, Robert, and me. We did not talk much, and he read a few articles, including one that quoted his brother in British Columbia as saying that Clyde would never cave in on his principles. I think it was at this point that the premier was finally able to assess how much he had conceded and how little everyone else had given. Shortly afterwards, he returned to the fifth floor. Hordes of officials had entered the conference room and were celebrating the deal with a few of the happier premiers, like David Peterson. I went in for a few minutes and spoke briefly to the premier and Robert, who looked as uncomfortable as I felt.

I then waited in the hall with Finkelstein for the final text and for the legal opinion regarding the distinct society clause, which was rumoured to be in preparation for annexing to the Accord. At this point, I began to sense that things were not *comme il faut*. There was a lot of activity, and people like Roger Tassé and Mary Dawson were looking preoccupied as they ran to and from various offices, but no paper was emerging. Then Finkelstein spoke to Maldoff and Carstairs, who were over in the Chateau Laurier, and discovered that Chrétien's team already had a copy of the draft opinion (presumably faxed over), while we on the fifth floor just outside the FPRO offices did not. I considered this a gross insult and could barely contain my anger. To compound the situation, Peter Mansbridge and the CBC team were already confidently announcing all the details of the agreement, which had already been leaked to them even though the situation within the Conference Centre was still in a state of flux.

The draft finally reached the premier's hands shortly before 11 p.m. He was still in the conference room; I was outside with Finkelstein. As I examined my copy, I was bitterly disappointed; it was worse than I had expected. The legal opinion had still not appeared, but at this point it was really immaterial to me. All its absence did was make a bad situation worse.

Then suddenly, everything changed. The premier angrily stormed out of the meeting room and announced that a critical clause was missing from the draft and that he would not be signing the agreement. Everyone and everything was thrown into confusion. As I scrambled to understand what had happened — I would not know all the details until a few minutes later — Finkelstein asked Wells for some instructions as to the legal opinion about the distinct society clause. Wells replied that he should carry on with any meeting with the officials about it, keeping in mind the premier's position, but that he himself was going back to the hotel immediately and would certainly not be signing any document. He then took Finkelstein into the conference room and introduced him to Mulroney and the federal officials — Tellier, Spector, Tassé, and Hartt. (The other premiers had left.) Finally, he marched across the street to the hotel with Robert, Judy, me, and a mob of reporters, leaving Finkelstein, with whom he would not speak again until the next day's breakfast meeting.

In his suite, we finally learned about the "missing clause." Apparently the premier and Frank McKenna had worked on a clause that would have committed the first ministers to assessing the impact of the distinct society clause on the Charter after a certain period of time and then pursuing appropriate constitutional amendments. This clause was certainly not great but at least it would have signalled that a couple of first ministers were conscious of the importance of our Charter rights and had established a minimal safeguard for them. The clause was to have read, "The Prime Minister and Premiers agree to cause a review of the advice to be conducted within ten years, and if jurisprudence over that period develops in a manner inconsistent with the advice given, the Prime Minister and Premiers are committed to seeking appropriate constitutional amendments."

When the draft was produced, however, that clause was missing. When the premier raised the issue, Mulroney apparently acknowledged its absence and asked Tassé what had happened. Tassé then had to admit to the premier that the Quebec delegation had vetoed it and that he had simply dropped it from the text. In a note to the premier the next day, Tassé further would state that in fact he had discussed the situation clearly with Tellier and Mulroney and that the federal officials had then decided to substitute another, more general provision for a periodic review of the entire Charter. So in fact, Mulroney had known exactly why it was no longer in the text when he responded to Wells's query, but had left it to Tassé to explain it.

The premier also related how Mulroney had desperately tried to have all premiers sign a copy of the agreement that night, ostensibly for his daughter Caroline's birthday, which was the next day or shortly thereafter. Apparently, eight of the premiers agreed; only Wells and Filmon refused. Mulroney's approach to constitutional negotiations left us all speechless.

In any event, the crunch had at least arrived, albeit three days later than I had first anticipated. The premier had finally been released from the pressure cooker. He now freely and openly denounced the entire process. As he explained to reporters while returning to the hotel, the missing clause, while an important trigger, had simply stripped the entire process and hence its product of any credibility.

While in the premier's suite, we watched some of the news coverage, which was still trumpeting the agreement and its details. What disappointed me the most was how ready Filmon now was to embrace the deal. (Carstairs's approval was absolutely no surprise and, given her close links to Chrétien's office, no longer of any consequence.) If, as I believed, Filmon and many of his closest advisors really had sincere doubts about the Accord, I would have expected him to leave himself some manoeuvring room to edge out if circumstances permitted. But he did not. As a result, the Accord would only be stopped in Manitoba by the likes of Elijah Harper and the literally thousands of people who signed up to make presentations at the province's legislative hearings.

The next day was Saturday. For the first time all week, the breakfast meeting took place in a serene atmosphere. It was finally sinking home, at least to me, that we were out of the vise. But of course it was by no means over. During breakfast the premier received a call from Mulroney about the missing clause. Since Quebec's veto meant that Mulroney could not possibly agree to reinsert the clause, I was fairly relaxed, and whatever Mulroney said had no impact on the premier. Further manipulation to get the premier to sign did not seem possible at this point.

Finkelstein reported that he had remained with the other officials until the early hours of the morning participating in drafting some of the legal language for the agreement. With respect to the missing clause, the Quebec delegation refused to add anything that would commit first ministers in advance to seek appropriate constitutional amendments should the distinct society clause be used to allow Quebec to override the Charter. The premier instructed Finkelstein to continue to participate in discussions that day, but only in a hands-off way and with the goal of protecting as well as possible Newfoundland's interest. The premier was not going to approve or recommend the deal and would now just bring it back to the province for a public examination. In the circumstances, this outcome was probably the best I could have envisaged, since the meeting would finally be over and we could all get out of the vortex. The court of public opinion would have the final word.

While entering the Conference Centre for the morning's first ministers' meeting, the premier made it clear to the mob of reporters massed outside that his dissatisfaction with the process and the deal went far beyond just the missing clause, although that had clearly been a catalyst. Mulroney then arrived and spent a full nine-and-a-half minutes standing on the sidewalk with Don Newman of CBC "Meechworld," trying to explain the missing clause as an unfortunate example of "occupational hazard." None of us could believe our ears!

At this point most of the delegation was with the premier in the small Newfoundland main floor office watching CBC Newsworld. The situation was in such a state of flux that no one knew exactly when the first ministers would start meeting. They finally convened in the late morning, again without Bourassa, who remained in the Chateau, adhering to his decision not to participate in any discussion of the distinct society clause. I spent some time on the fifth floor, where the atmosphere was extremely subdued. All I recall, besides small talk, is Frank McKenna emerging once to find out the baseball scores. I then returned to the main floor office.

About noon, the premier and Filmon suddenly appeared at the door. They had left the meeting and then decided to confer privately over lunch. They immediately walked over to the premier's room in the Chateau. Filmon did not want the premier to return to the conference room for his papers, in case he was sidetracked by the other premiers, so Paul Dicks went in to retrieve them and the two of us walked over to the premier's room. After sending the papers in, we waited outside the door with the at least twenty reporters who were camped in the hall and around the elevators, desperate for any news. The meeting ended around 2:30 p.m.

Once more I could not be sure exactly what Filmon and Wells had discussed. I was hoping that overnight Filmon had had second thoughts about his decision to support the new deal. Some of Manitoba's advisors were also assuming that since Wells had stuck with Filmon throughout the week, that Filmon would stick with Wells during this final stage.

The meeting of all the premiers would not recommence until close to 4 p.m. This time Bourassa would attend. Until it started, we sat with Wells in the Newfoundland office talking about the conference in general terms. The premier then worked on a few notes for his closing remarks. He seemed fairly relaxed and said he looked forward to leaving. The only unusual thing I recall was that the Prime Minister's Office called Finkelstein to ask him if he wanted to go upstairs and have his picture taken with Mulroney. Finkelstein declined.

Finkelstein had continued to participate in a minor way in the legal opinion that was to be annexed to the agreement and spoke to Wells about it. The premier seemed uninterested, but told Finkelstein that although he personally could not endorse it, Finkelstein was free to sign if he wanted. Finkelstein then indicated that, like Manitoba's legal advisors, he would not sign it.

The first ministers' meeting dragged on for almost three hours while we all asked ourselves what on earth could be taking so long. Finally, about 7 p.m., the premier emerged to discuss with us what sort of formal qualification he should attach to the new deal to indicate that he was agreeing only to take it back to Newfoundland to put it to the people. Frank McKenna in particular seemed anxious to have the premier sign the same document as everyone else, however conditionally. It appeared that Filmon had already been persuaded to do so, although he made it clear that final acceptance would depend on the results of public hearings in Manitoba. Both Paul Dicks and I spoke to Wells. Dicks argued that since the premier was in no way approving the deal and was committed to taking it back to Newfoundland and Labrador for meaningful discussion, he must not sign the same document. If he did, it would send out the wrong signals to the public and probably be manipulated in some way by the feds.

Dicks spoke intently to the premier and discussed the proviso that ultimately appeared below the premier's conditional signature. Unfortunately, he could not offset the influence of Frank McKenna, who emerged from the conference room to join us and, with a "come on, Clyde" approach, continually pressed him at least to sign the same document, even if it had a proviso attached. The premier finally agreed.

Our fears of being manipulated soon proved valid. At about 10 p.m. the prime minister at last convened an open first ministers' meeting, though only for closing statements. It was outrageously staged. In the large Conference Centre hall, all the premiers and their justice or intergovernmental affairs ministers were sitting around the table when what seemed to be the full federal cabinet rushed in to sit behind the prime minister, who arrived last, accompanied by Lowell Murray and Norman Spector. Then Spector very ostentatiously took the single agreement around for everyone's signature.

To outside observers and to many media, it appeared that all was sweetness and harmony and that everyone had agreed to the new deal. Anyone listening closely, however, would have heard Wells eloquently and cogently give the reasons why he was not approving the new agreement, but was only taking it back for consideration by the people of his province. Indeed, the proviso under his signature said clearly that he was only undertaking to submit the Meech Lake Accord "for appropriate legislative or public consideration and to use every possible effort to achieve a decision prior to June 23, 1990." And it added that only if Meech was legislatively or publicly approved would he then endorse fully the most recent 1990 agreement.

Unfortunately, the provisos were in rather arcane legal language and perhaps not easily understood by many observers. One result was that early on Sunday, June 10, the *Ottawa Sun* ran a gloating front page picture of Mulroney with a screaming headline: "It's a deal!"

The premier spoke first by prior agreement with Mulroney. (Usual protocol would have had him speak last, since he was premier of the youngest province.) The other premiers' speeches were lengthy, tedious, and self-congratulatory. I was exhausted and had a definite sense that I was watching a theatre of the absurd. By 1 or 2 a.m. the ordeal was finally over. We were out of the vortex and the final countdown was on.

ELEVEN

The Final Manipulation

FTER BARELY THREE HOURS' SLEEP, the premier, Robert Dornan, Judy Foote, Paul Dicks, Walter Noel, and I were all out at the airport at 6 a.m. on June 10 to take the tiny King-Air jet back to St. John's. Conversation was subdued with some light relief provided by a selection of photographs Mulroney had given the premier at the conclusion of the meeting. Apparently his official photographer had been present throughout, snapping pictures at every opportunity, even during the most serious discussions. I leave it to others to conclude what this says about our prime minister, but I think it is the height of absurdity.

The premier and I also had some time to discuss the writing of a referendum question. I had drafted some possible alternatives several weeks earlier. As he had indicated clearly in his remarks the previous night, he favoured a referendum on the Accord in Newfoundland and Labrador. The only concern was whether there was time to hold one before June 23.

In this connection, as early as March 22, when the motion to rescind was introduced, the premier had been advised by officials that a referendum vote could take place on fourteen days' notice. He had referred to this advice a number of times in media interviews; so had I during, for example, a less-than-pleasant off-the-record discussion with a *Le Devoir* correspondent who was obviously trying to create the line that we were not really serious about a referendum. In fact, the motion to rescind was introduced and passed as soon as possible after the reopening of the House on March 8, precisely so that there would be enough time for a referendum.

We landed at the St. John's airport in mid-afternoon. Edsel Bonnell and a few others came out to the tarmac to meet us and to alert the premier that several hundred people were in the airport to welcome him back and congratulate him for hanging tough and surviving the ordeal in Ottawa. The crowd was enthusiastic, which clearly reassured the premier. At one point while he was speaking to them, his voice broke and it was plain how relieved he was that the tension-filled Ottawa conference was finally over.

One of the premier's special assistants gave me a lift back to the office. I had a strange, shell-shocked feeling when I arrived and realized that we had been away a full seven days, rather than the mere two or three I had expected. I had difficulty placing events in perspective from my St. John's base.

The premier had scheduled a cabinet meeting as soon as possible after his arrival to discuss the next course of action. Just before going into the meeting, he asked me to do a quick memo comparing the Meech Lake Accord with the proposed new agreement and the primary concerns of Newfoundland. This was not difficult to do and was a good way to demonstrate how minimal the so-called companion resolution was. This memo was later distributed to the Liberal caucus. I knew then that the premier could not himself endorse either the resolution or the Accord.

The premier decided to call a press conference for early in the evening. He also issued a press release explaining exactly what he had signed and stating unequivocally that none of Newfoundland's primary concerns had been addressed in the companion resolution. He seemed tired, but also relaxed and extremely clear about his views.

The cabinet debate over whether a referendum or a free vote would be held continued the next morning. In the early afternoon, the premier announced that because of the time constraints — eleven days were not enough to organize a referendum — a free vote would have to be held instead. This meant that all MHAs would shortly return to their districts to consult their constituents and return for the legislative debate, which would start on Wednesday, June 20.

That very same day, the prime minister was giving his infamous "roll the dice" interview to *Globe and Mail* reporters Jeffrey Simpson, Graham Fraser, and Susan Delacourt. It appeared the next day, Tuesday, June 12, on the front page. In it, Mulroney made it clear that he had deliberately timed the first ministers' meeting to ensure a crisis atmosphere, to maximize pressure on the hold-out provinces, and to preclude the holding of a referendum in Newfoundland. Till then, it had always been claimed that the delay was a result of uncertainty as to whether there was sufficient "common ground" among opponents to the Accord to justify a meeting. Mulroney's revelation was not particularly surprising to those familiar with his overwhelmingly "political" approach to matters, but his bluntness on this occasion was extraordinary. He said that he and his advisors had gathered at 24 Sussex Drive a month before the June meeting to map out the federal strategy. "Right here, I told them when it would be," Mulroney said. "I told them a month ago when we were going to [meet]. It's like an election campaign. You count backward. [I said] that's the day we're going to roll the dice."

The reaction in Newfoundland was electric. The lead editorial in the St. John's Evening *Telegram* demanded in outrage that the premier revoke his invitation to Mulroney to address the House of Assembly. (The premier had extended this invitation to all first ministers in the context of the free-vote debate so that they could offer their views of why the Accord had to be passed.) Telephone calls from Newfoundlanders soon flooded the premier's switchboard. One irate gentleman, who worked at the airport, called to say that he was not going to let the prime minister's plane onto the tarmac if he decided to come to speak to the MHAs.

For the remaining days of the debate, I co-ordinated responses to the over 12,000 letters and faxes that arrived during the ten-day period. The fax machine literally went non-stop twenty-four hours a day for the remaining days down to June 23. One gentleman from British Columbia called to say that it had taken him three days to get through. Likewise, the phones never stopped ringing with calls from across Canada, and we brought in four or five young people to help answer them. They were also instructed to pass on to the callers any basic information such as the lists of MHAs, since with a free vote pending it was necessary now to convey their sentiments not just to the premier but to all elected members. Ninety-five percent of all the calls and letters we received supported the premier, which is the most tangible demonstration of how out of touch the other first ministers were with the wishes of Canadians at this critical juncture.

I also spent a good part of my time addressing ongoing crises and trying to counter the spins being generated, mainly in Ottawa and Toronto, that the premier really wanted his MHAs to hold their noses and vote in favour of the Accord. I was always convinced that the premier would vote against the Accord and that during the free-vote debate he would make an animated and inspiring speech exposing its flaws and setting out his well-reasoned arguments for reopening negotiations. But he was scrupulous in his efforts to ensure a free vote and refused to answer any express questions as to how he would vote. This only aided the spin doctors.

As I noted earlier, some of the most serious misstatements came through Brian Tobin on behalf of the Chrétien team. For example, Tobin told the Liberal caucus in Ottawa that he had been an advisor to the premier during the week of the negotiations and that the premier obviously wanted the Accord to pass since he had not walked out of the conference. When I relayed this to the premier on Wednesday, June 13, just before he flew out to his district in Corner Brook, he was extremely angry. He asked me to call Tobin directly, but later decided to get Edsel to do it. Edsel spoke to Tobin later that day and indicated to him clearly that such fabrications were to be ended immediately.

By now, Jean Chrétien was in an awkward position. He would remain basically incommunicado until June 22, except for a very brief phone call with the premier on June 13, to which I was privy. The premier was courteous as always; he indicated to him that his leadership rivals, Sheila Copps and Paul Martin, were coming out to argue the case for the Accord on hot-line shows in St. John's on June 15 and that he, too, was welcome to come out. Chrétien refused the invitation — yet further proof that he was no longer opposed to the Accord and wanted to lie low. Not surprisingly, the callers to the June 15 hot line were vehemently in favour of reopening the Accord, which made it obvious that whatever Copps and Martin thought was irrelevant — the people stood firmly behind the premier.

Indeed, the amount of support the premier received, both personally and for his position on the Accord, was phenomenal throughout the debate. The desperate forays of federal cabinet ministers into almost every corner of the province after the rescission motion was introduced in March had absolutely no impact. And pro-Meechers were roundly condemned whenever they ventured onto the local radio talk-shows to criticize the premier. One of many examples of this was the outrage levelled at Jean Charest on March 23, when he made the ill-advised comment on Bill Rowe's show that the premier, in providing for a referendum, was "hiding behind the skirts of the people." It would be difficult to think of anything more certain to provoke a backlash among listeners.

So I remained optimistic about the course of events in Newfoundland and Labrador. By this time, even more encouraging news was coming out of Manitoba. Shortly after returning to Winnipeg, Filmon had introduced the motion to approve Meech and the companion resolution, and had asked the legislature for unanimous agreement to shorten the time for the mandatory public hearings so that there could be a vote by June 23. But there was a procedural problem requiring a second introduction of the motion; and later, on Tuesday, June 12, the lone aboriginal representative, Elijah Harper, strongly backed by aboriginal groups across Canada, denied the legislature the unanimous consent required for debate. Harper then proceeded to run out the clock on the Accord. While this was going on, the list of people who wanted to appear at the Manitoba hearings was lengthening daily; it would hold over 5,000 names by the time the deadline expired.

The resolve of the aboriginal leaders was encouraging and entirely appropriate. Few were better placed to lead the opposition than the first inhabitants of Canada, who, as so many people pointed out, were surely as important, distinctive, and fundamental as any other group. They put an abrupt end to the naïve expectations that their opposition could be effectively bought off by the minimal concession in the companion resolution stipulating mandatory first ministers' conferences on aboriginal concerns every three years. Indeed, they were justifiably insulted by the companion resolution.

Shortly after returning to St. John's, I had an interesting conversation with Georges Erasmus of the Assembly of First Nations, John Amagoalik of the Inuit Tapirisat of Canada and Chris McCormick of the Native Council of Canada. Erasmus called me from Ottawa where they were meeting, and we talked on the speaker phone. They pointed out bluntly that the legal opinion annexed to the companion resolution in fact took away what little protection the aboriginal groups had in the Accord. The Accord at least stipulated that the distinct society clause did not affect aboriginal rights in the Charter, or Parliament's legislative jurisdiction in respect of "Indians and Lands reserved for the Indians." Yet the legal opinion did not repeat this prior provision and by implication seemed to contradict it. This assessment was well-founded, and I could only agree with their analysis. Erasmus wrote a letter on June 11 stating his concerns to Peter Hogg, one of the signatories of the opinion. Hogg wrote back on June 13 to confirm that the opinion's authors had not intended to take away from the Meech provision. Even so, this demonstrates the complete neglect of aboriginal issues in the hot-house atmosphere in Ottawa. It also demonstrates how critical it will be in the future to broaden the process of constitutional reform so that it takes into account the interests of *everyone*.

In a final desperate attempt to eliminate the aboriginal opposition, Mulroney sent his top advisors to meet with the Manitoba chiefs on Monday, June 18. They brought a letter from the prime minister proposing a number of Band-Aid solutions, including a royal commission on aboriginal concerns. Reports indicate that the meeting lasted all of twenty minutes and that Lowell Murray, among others, was left speechless.

On Monday and Tuesday, June 18 and 19, Wells joined the Quebec and Maritime premiers in Mystic, Connecticut, for the annual regional meeting of premiers and state governors. In the meantime, in St. John's, MHAs were beginning to return from their districts and tensions were building in anticipation of the legislative debates, which were scheduled to start on Wednesday.

An extraordinary number of people flew to St. John's from as far away as Vancouver to lend moral support to the premier and stay for the final vote. Of course, not all of these were welcome. One person in particular was not: Archie Pafford, the leader of the intolerant and anti-bilingual Confederation of Regions party in New Brunswick. I was alerted that he was on his way to give the premier a petition indicating his party's strong support. In turn, I alerted Edsel, Margie, and Rosie not to allow him at any time to meet with the premier. All the premier needed at this point was to be identified, however wrongly, with an anti-Quebec, anti-bilingual lobby — the pro-Meechers would have a field day. Unfortunately, Pafford arrived at the office unexpectedly, and one of the special assistants brought him inside for a small tour. When Pafford was introduced to me, I was very abrupt with him, indicating that the premier certainly did not share his reasons for wanting to reject the Accord. Much to the surprise of the special assistant, I then escorted Pafford to the exit. Needless to say, he was annoyed. He returned a little while later to complain about my treatment. This time Robert dealt with him, probably less abruptly, though no less firmly.

At this point the pro-Meech tactics were getting nasty. Federal MPs like John Crosbie were personally phoning all Newfoundland MHAs to urge them to vote for the Accord, over the premier's protest that this compromised the free vote. Scare tactics were also being used, with Tory MPs and MHAs alleging that Wells's opposition would lead to the break-up of Canada, the loss of old-age pensions, and so on. At one point, I received a call from an elderly man asking me if it was true that he would lose his pension.

Meanwhile, the airwaves were supersaturated with Meech, day and night. Perhaps the most memorable video bite appeared on a "Journal" documentary that followed a House of Assembly member around in his quest to solicit the views of fishermen in his district. One busy fisherman replied that he did not think Meech Lake was good for Canada. When asked whether he was worried that Quebec might separate if Meech failed, he replied in a devastatingly straightforward manner, "Separate? But where would they go?" It was a classic.

The debate in the House of Assembly opened on Wednesday, June 20. The premier was to speak last, on June 22, but I was able to reassure anxious callers that all MHAs would clearly know which way the premier was going to vote before the vote actually took place. (Many pundits were already speculating that if Wells voted last, the Accord might pass, since some waverers on the government side would vote in favour of it, whereas they would likely be persuaded to stick with the premier if he came out against it before they cast their vote.) In any event, I also continually reassured people that the premier would make a firm speech that would leave no doubt as to which way he would vote at the end.

I never went up to the House of Assembly to watch the speeches, but I was able to listen to all of them in my office over the PA system. I probably would not have been able to get into the House very easily: the galleries were packed with media and observers. Premiers Peterson, McKenna, and Devine had all accepted the invitation to address the House, as had the prime minister. Peterson and McKenna spoke on June 20. Both men repeated their standard positions and, as it turned out, did not sway any members. The national media of course accorded most of its coverage to them. Even so, at every opportunity I would emphasize to others that the speeches of the Liberal MHAs were far more important. Most of these were eloquent and well-reasoned analyses of why they could not support the Accord in its present form.

Late in the evening of June 20, the premier called me up to the office on the House of Assembly floor in the Confederation Building. He said he wanted to draft a possible amendment to the constitutional amending procedure to eliminate any single province's right of veto. I couldn't understand the purpose of this, but he considered that it might be helpful to put it forward to show that he was willing to give up Newfoundland's veto, even though at that time, under the Accord, Newfoundland had the right to kill the Accord. Professor Stephen Scott of McGill University Law School happened to be there; after meeting with the premier and me, he put something into legal language. I spoke in favour of ensuring that in any such proposal for a new amending formula, there would be a referendum mechanism, and the premier eventually agreed to this. I still saw no need for this last-minute proposal and was relieved to find that the initiative was vetoed by the Liberal caucus when it met early the next morning.

Devine and the prime minister addressed the House of Assembly on Thursday, June 21. Like Peterson and McKenna, they repeated their standard pro-Meech arguments. Mulroney, in particular, avoided any discussion of the Accord's substance; in his usual facile manner, he simply argued that it had to pass or there would be incalculable consequences.

That week, the prestigious British magazine *The Economist* ran an excellent lead editorial bluntly criticizing the Accord for the balkanizing instrument it was and accusing Mulroney of appeasing Quebec. The timing was perfect, and Robert and I made sure that copies were made and distributed to all MHAs on Thursday morning. Incredibly, the opposition claimed that the premier was unfairly trying to manipulate the vote. This, at a time when Crosbie was camped outside the House of Assembly buttonholing Liberal MHAs and making veiled threats of federal retribution if the Accord failed!

Later that day, Donald Blenkarn, the ever bumptious and unpredictable Ontario Tory MP, was reported as saying that Newfoundland should be towed out to sea and sunk. This remark was almost as ill-advised as the one by Quebec MP Denis Pronovost, shortly before the June meeting, that the premier was a "mental case," or the one from Joe Clark calling the premier an "egomaniac." All these statements went over like lead balloons. In Newfoundland particularly, they had the completely unintended effect of strengthening the premier's support and the determination of government members to oppose the Accord.

The premier had dinner with Mulroney at his home and then returned to the House at 9 p.m. for the evening session. He did not reveal the details of that dinner conversation but did say that he told Mulroney that he believed that the Accord would be rejected. By then, there had been at least three defections, including the cabinet minister responsible for conducting Chrétien's campaign in Newfoundland, David Gilbert. This was not enough to upset the Liberal majority — at least seven shifts were required — and I remained fully confident that the vote would reject the Accord.

After the 11 p.m. adjournment, the premier met with most but not all of the members of caucus in the government common room. They discussed the very real possibility that Elijah Harper was going to prevent the Manitoba debate from proceeding one last time the next day, Friday, June 22. Once this happened, the Accord would die in Manitoba since the Manitoba legislature would then be closed for the weekend and would not reopen until after the June 23 deadline.

According to the premier, the caucus also discussed the probability that the vote in Newfoundland would reject the Accord. He added that the general feeling of caucus was that a vote in Newfoundland against the Accord, would do nothing but harm if the Accord had by then effectively been spiked in Manitoba. The overwhelming view of caucus was that if the process could not be completed in Manitoba, the debate in Newfoundland should be adjourned without a vote.

Late that night Wells spoke to Filmon, who indicated that it was a virtual certainty that the Manitoba legislature would adjourn on Friday at 12:30 p.m. — 3 p.m. Newfoundland time — because of the inability to get unanimous consent to proceed.

On Friday morning, June 22, the House of Assembly met at 9 a.m. instead of 10 a.m. in order to deal with a major labour dispute. The Meech Lake debate resumed shortly after 10 a.m. I was on edge, but also convinced that if a vote were held it would clearly reject the Accord.

A couple of phone calls during the morning involving the premier turned out to be critical. I was not present, but the premier subsequently set out the precise details of them in a press release so that it would be emphatically clear why he ultimately decided not to hold the free vote. At about 10 a.m. Wells phoned John Crosbie and told him he was concerned about the consequences of the Newfoundland legislature voting to reject the Accord after Manitoba had failed to approve it. He expressed the opinion that such a vote would do no good and probably would cause harm and resentment. Crosbie seemed impressed by the comments and said he would speak with his colleagues in Ottawa and get back to Wells.

At 10:30 a.m. Lowell Murray returned an earlier call from the premier, who told him of his conversation with Crosbie. Murray urged Wells to proceed with the vote. Wells recounted his conversation with Filmon and restated his view that a vote in Newfoundland in such circumstances would be both pointless and harmful. Murray then told him that the feds felt there was a possible way around the problem in Manitoba. Wells asked what it was. Murray replied that they were looking at a dozen or more proposals, and that while a firm decision had not been taken, they were leaning toward a reference to the Supreme Court of Canada for an opinion that the start of the three-year time period could be deferred to September 1990. That month was three years after Saskatchewan, the first province after Quebec, approved the Accord. (Quebec would have to reapprove the Accord.)

When Wells questioned him about this point, Murray told him he had several opinions, but could not give Wells details at this particular time. Wells told him that in that case it would be best to defer the vote in Newfoundland because it was virtually certain to be rejected if the vote were to be taken at that stage, which would make the reference to the Supreme Court utterly useless. Murray argued that the feds felt they would only be able to ask the Court for an opinion if the Accord had been passed by all provinces other than Manitoba since in Manitoba at least there was a commitment by the leaders to see the Accord passed. Wells told him he disagreed and that the Court would decide this on the basis of the legal issues involved, not on the question of whether or not there were political undertakings of provinces that had not yet ratified the Accord. He added that if the federal government could extend the time for Manitoba, they could also extend it for Newfoundland.

Wells emphasized again that the reference to the Supreme Court could only be useful if Newfoundland adjourned its debate, without a vote for the time being, because a vote on that day would certainly result in a rejection. Murray told Wells he would discuss the matter and get back to him.

About noon, Elijah Harper called Wells and told him that he was going to prevent the Manitoba legislature from proceeding and that he was determined to prevent approval of the Accord. It was now clear that Meech would die in Manitoba at about 3 p.m. Newfoundland time.

After the 1 p.m. adjournment of the House of Assembly, the Liberal caucus met. Wells advised the caucus of the situation in Manitoba and the discussions with Crosbie and Murray, from whom he was still waiting to hear. Caucus decided that it was best not to take a vote in light of the fact that the matter had come to an end in Manitoba. Most members felt very strongly about this; however, they did give Wells and the government house leader, Winston Baker, the discretion to proceed with the vote depending on the response from Murray and/or Crosbie.

When Wells had still not heard from either Murray or Crosbie by 1:30 p.m., he asked Margie to place a call to Murray. Margie was told that Murray was there and was asked to get Wells on the line. When Wells answered the phone, Murray's secretary asked him to hold on for a moment while she found the senator. When she returned, she apologized, saying he was just leaving the office and would not be able to speak to Wells after all.

A few minutes before the premier called Murray's office, I received a call from a friend in Ottawa, who told me that someone she knew had just been rushed into the CTV studio to provide immediate commentary on a press conference summoned by Murray. We all crowded into Edsel's office to watch Newsworld. I was numbed to what I now heard: the premier had just been trying to get through to Murray, and Murray was now ambushing the premier with a press conference. I could not disguise my disbelief that he was calmly announcing that the federal government had found a way to extend the deadline to accommodate the Manitoba hearings, but that it would only work if Newfoundland approved the Accord! Murray said that the federal government would apply to the Supreme Court of Canada for a declaration that would allow the deadline to be deferred until September, but that if Newfoundland voted to defeat the Accord, this would not be possible.

The immediate reaction of Wells and all of us in the office, which was supported by messages that began arriving immediately over the grinding fax machine, was that what could be done for Manitoba could also be done for Newfoundland and that there was no reason why Newfoundland now should not hold its referendum. For the premier, as he stated firmly in his speech a couple of hours later, the federal tactic was "the final manipulation." The feds had deliberately stepped up the pressure on Newfoundland MHAs and targeted them unfairly as the villains who killed Meech.

Wells was livid. After a quick discussion with the caucus members who were available, he stated that everyone agreed that Murray's initiative put Newfoundland in an untenable position. The members of the caucus agreed that the debate must be adjourned in the Newfoundland House, and that the voting must be deferred unless and until the federal government obtained a ruling from the Supreme Court of Canada that the three-year time period could be extended.

Wells immediately advised the opposition leader, Tom Rideout, that he intended to move for the adjournment of the debate. He also told Rideout about the unaccountable failure of both Murray and Crosbie to get back to him. At the suggestion of Len Simms, the opposition house leader, the opening of the House was adjourned so that a meeting could be arranged with Rideout, Simms, Crosbie, Baker, and Wells.

That meeting took place in the Speaker's office. When Wells complained that Crosbie had not gotten back to him, Crosbie replied, "I could not get back to you because they did not get back to me." Wells told Crosbie that in light of Murray's actions, he intended to move for adjournment, because Murray's manipulation had placed Newfoundland in an untenable position. He added that the reference to the Supreme Court of Canada could only be worthwhile if the vote in Newfoundland was deferred, because such a vote, if taken on that day, would certainly result in a rejection. Both Rideout and Simms agreed that the Newfoundland vote would likely be for rejection of the Accord. Crosbie acknowledged that it was also his view. He therefore agreed that he would call the prime minister and get back to Wells as quickly as possible.

While Crosbie was making that call, the debate in the House resumed. After the last opposition member to speak, other than the opposition leader, concluded her remarks, the House again recessed briefly to allow for a meeting with Crosbie. Again Rideout, Simms, Baker and Wells attended. Crosbie advised them that he had been speaking with the prime minister and said the federal government would approve of the debate being adjourned, without a vote being taken, and would ensure that Newfoundland was treated the same as Manitoba, if Wells would agree to state publicly, as Filmon had done, that he would in the future support the Meech Lake Accord. Wells told Crosbie that this was blackmail and he would not give in to it.

The members of the liberal caucus who were then available reconfirmed their view that it was in the best interest of the nation and the province that the present debate in Newfoundland be adjourned without a vote. Thus, at the direction of caucus, Wells put forward the motion to adjourn following a lengthy, riveting speech eloquently restating his concerns with the accord and venting his anger with Murray, Crosbie, and Mulroney's manipulations and fear-mongering. At about 8:30 p.m., the House voted in favour of the motion, thereby deferring — likely forever — the vote on the Meech Lake Accord. All the Liberal MHAs supported the motion.

With Edsel and a couple of others, I watched the final vote on Newsworld. Despite Edsel's exasperated reminders, "It's over, Debbie, it's over," I could not believe it was finally finished. I watched anxiously as Lowell Murray emerged from a meeting with Mulroney a few moments later to speak to the press. I expected further devious tactics. Instead, Murray stood before the microphone, held up a copy of the June 1990 agreement, pointed to the premier's signature, and complained that the premier had not lived up to his commitment. Nothing could have been more absurd. The finger-pointing continues to this day.

THE PREMIER AND MRS. WELLS came down to the office for a few minutes after the final vote to adjourn. The mood was subdued. Both spoke briefly on the phone in my office to a Canadian serviceman, who was calling all the way from Lahr, West Germany, to pass on his congratulations. The fax machine was constantly on the go. Even at 10 p.m., we still had three students helping us to handle the phone lines.

Except that he looked tired, the premier showed no signs of the relentless pressure he had been under. As I started to reflect on the last few weeks, I was relieved that at least from my perspective, he had been able to maintain his integrity and demonstrate clearly that principles and openness can win against games and devious tactics. It now seemed incredible that the pro-Meechers had almost succeeded in grinding down a person as strong as the premier, and I had to remind myself that only less than four weeks earlier I had resigned myself to the likelihood that there would be a deal. But Mulroney's roll of the dice had failed.

On Saturday morning, June 23, I woke in time to watch the televised statements of Bourassa and Mulroney. I was still apprehensive about some last-minute tactic despite Edsel Bonnell's reassurances the night before that the ordeal was over.

Both statements were predictable, and both were full of hollow and self-righteous indignation. I was under no illusions as to what was ahead: inevitably Mulroney and his nationalist-dominated Quebec caucus would try again; meanwhile, Bourassa would retire into splendid isolation from Canadian affairs and continue his own dance with the nationalists. All one could hope for now was that the Meech experience would ensure open, principled debate that was based clearly on respect for the sovereignty of the Canadian people, and that a repeat of the most recent debacle could be avoided.

Early Saturday morning, the premier and his wife flew out to the Liberal leadership convention in Calgary and stayed on for a brief holiday. For the next few days I tried to cope with the correspondence that continued to swamp the office. I also decided to try to "de-meech" myself by getting away to some place that would help me to remember all the absurdities of our constitutional debate. My choice was Peru. I flew to Lima on July 2 with my knapsack and no itinerary. Edsel's parting comment was that if a constitutional crisis erupted while I was there, he would know who was behind it. He was joking, but as it turned out, the country was traversing a severe crisis that would soon lead to the suspension of all civil liberties.

As I expected, by travelling in Peru and in Bolivia as well, I was able to put the Meech debate in its proper perspective. Especially in Peru, people are so desperately poor that they will use a knife to slash open your knapsack to steal what little might be in it. Young homeless people regularly die in the streets at night from the cold or from unnatural causes. Terrorists deliberately fuel people's insecurity and fear for the future by assassinating local leaders and disrupting water and electricity supplies. Street vendors riot in the hope of acquiring licences to sell.

Whenever I mentioned that I came from Canada, I could see the envy and admiration light up people's eyes. I left Peru as internal tensions were rapidly escalating, just a few days before the newly installed government declared martial law and suspended all civil liberties. I clearly remember thinking how lucky I was to be returning to Canada.

I stayed on for another year in St. John's as the Director of Constitutional Policy. I then joined an economic consulting firm in Ottawa in order to work on a special "Economics of Confederation" project.

Since the Meech Lake Accord's failure, Canadians have witnessed a string of commissions, hearings, and reports, of which the Bélanger-Campeau Commission in Quebec, the Spicer Commission, the Quebec Liberal Party's Allaire Report, and, most recently, the Beaudoin-Dobbie Special Joint Committee are only the most prominent. Yet, only two years after the death of Meech, we are again in the middle of another manufactured constitutional crisis, when most Canadians would prefer their leaders to focus their attention on the desperate state of the economy. All the same issues, tensions, and games are resurfacing in much the same form as during the Meech Lake debate. Once again our national leadership and self-appointed constitutional élites have collapsed in the face of Quebec's demands for more powers and a Charter override; once again they are going through contortions in an attempt to figure out how to give away federal powers and cripple the ability to establish minimum national standards.

And many of the same people are still prominently involved: Roger Tassé is busy advising the federal government while Eric Maldoff and Eddie Goldenberg are busy advising Liberal leader Jean Chrétien. Claude Castonguay, a Conservative senator, briefly co-chaired the Special Parliamentary Committee. Ghislain Dufour and the other members of the Quebec business élite are busy pushing decentralization and special status for Quebec, as are his counterparts at the national level, such as Thomas d'Aquino and the Business Council on National Issues. Pro-Meech academics are well-entrenched advising the Federal-Provincial Relations Office. A few key people have of course changed positions or roles. Several of the "Meech premiers" — David Peterson, Bill Vander Zalm, and Grant Devine — have been voted out of office, while John Buchanan has been bumped up to the Senate. Gary Filmon, however, finally won his majority as premier of Manitoba, while Sharon Carstairs, a convert to Meech, lost her role as opposition leader. Norman Spector moved over to replace Stanley Hartt as Mulroney's chief of staff, but quickly moved on to become Ambassador to Israel. Lowell Murray was moved from the constitutional affairs portfolio in favour of Joe "Community of Communities" Clark.

As we now head into the last stages of the debate leading up to the Quebec referendum deadline, obvious parallels with the Meech Lake debate continue to multiply: the Beaudoin-Dobbie Report, in its desperate scramble for unanimity, recalls the abortive Charest Report; the Quebec National Assembly's "disapproval" of that report is similar to its condemnation in early April 1990 of any attempt at a companion resolution to amend Meech; and the proposals — whatever they turn out to be — will be "unbundled" or "severed" so that certain parts can be passed with the approval of only seven provinces and the federal government. It remains to be seen whether what happened in June 1990 was really "the final manipulation."

INDEX

Aboriginal peoples, 18, 71, 72, 139-40

Add-ons to the Accord, proposed, 46, 58, 82, 90, 91, 99-100, 106, 109, 112, 119-20

Alberta: Wells's speeches and meetings in, 62-63, 64

Allaire, Jean, 67

Amending formula, 3, 4, 18-19, 31, 60-61

Association for the Protection of English in Canada (APEC), 66, 67

Association in Favour of Meech Lake, 53- 54, 56

Beaudoin-Dobbie Report, 151

Bilingualism, 5, 44, 45, 67

Bill 178, 67, 86

Blakeney, Allan, 8-9

Blenkarn, Donald, 143

Blondin, Ethel, 84, 88

Bonnell, Edsel, 10, 16, 35, 136, 138, 147

Bouchard, Lucien, 78, 90, 91, 91

Bourassa, Robert, 53, 75, 78, 149; inflexibility on amendments to Meech, 20, 77; at June 1990 meeting, 104, 110, 113, 121, 125, 132, 133

Brinkmanship, 2, 56, 100, 101, 109, 137

British Columbia: Wells's meetings in, 63-64. *See also* Vander Zalm, William

Buchanan, John, 104, 128, 151

Bureaucracy, 12, 22-24, 38, 40-41

Business Council on National Issues (BCNI), 54, 96, 151

Canada clause, 18, 27, 87-88, 106, 110, 114, 118, 119, 120, 125

Canada West Foundation, 62

Canadian Coalition on the Constitution, 7

Canadians for a Unifying Constitution, 54, 58, 96

Carstairs, Sharon, 16, 88, 114, 115, 123, 124, 125, 131, 151

Castonguay, Claude, 53, 54, 55, 56, 151

CBC Newsworld, 35, 41, 78-79, 132, 145- 46

Charest, Jean, 80, 84, 139

Charest Committee, 80-91; Report, 88-89; Wells's presentation before, 82-84

Charter of Rights and Freedoms, 19, 20, 32-33, 87

Chrétien, Jean, 31, 51-52, 87, 88, 89- 90, 94, 95, 114, 123, 138, 151

Churchill Falls power contract, 75, 104

Clark, Joe, 151

"Closed-door" approach to constitutional reform, 14

Cohen, Andrew, 46

Conseil du Patronat du Québec (CPQ), 55, 103

Constitution Act, 1982, 28, 83, 87-88

Correspondence on Meech, 44-45, 47-48, 66, 79, 137, 151

Crosbie, John, 141, 143, 144, 146, 147

Cullen-Couture Agreement, 74

D'Aquino, Thomas, 54, 58, 151

Dawson, Mary, 101, 116

Decore, Laurence, 62

Dennison, Don, 22, 23, 72

Devine, Grant, 64, 142, 151

Dicks, Paul, 14, 46, 103, 127, 132, 133, 134

Distinct society clause, 3, 17, 18, 32- 33, 51, 72, 83, 85-86, 110-11, 115-16, 118-20, 129, 130; suggestion to recast as preamble, 26-27, 33, 109

Dornan, Robert, 8, 9, 50, 83-84

Dufour, Ghislain, 54-55, 151

Economist, The, 142

Efford, John, 74

English-only resolutions, 66-67

Erasmus, Georges, 139, 140

Federal powers, 3, 4, 11-12, 14, 17, 18- 19, 28, 47

Federal-provincial conferences. *See* First Ministers' Conferences